ENDORSEMENTS

"A New Lens is a collection of love letters from God that would have remained unopened and forgotten had Kathy Gray stayed in her theological lane. Instead, she courageously steps out, offering a biblically grounded, life-giving exploration of dream interpretation. Through over a dozen destiny-shaping encounters with God, Kathy shows that dreams are not just fleeting images, but vital messages from the heart of the Father. Whether you're a dreamer or not, this book will stir your faith to believe that God can—and will—speak to you through your dreams."

Michael and Amanda Wise

Amanda Wise
Former Executive Assistant to the late John Paul Jackson
Guest Coordinator at Daystar Television Network

Michael Wise
Former VP of Operations for Streams Ministries
Co-Author of The 20 Categories of Dreams
Writer/Producer of Dreams & Mysteries (Season 1)

"Kathy Gray has a unique voice that brings sound Biblical wisdom and a love for how God speaks in a very conversational way. It feels like you are sitting across the table from her having a cup of coffee discussing the ways of God. She has brought together her experience, her own study of the Bible, and principles she has learned along her journey from others into an easy to read and understand book. Anyone that desires to learn a biblical lens for dreams and how God shares the meaning of them will find this book treasure."

John E. Thomas
President
Streams Ministries Intl

"Kathy's personal relationship with God and her deep knowledge of scripture enables her to help interpret the messages He conveys through dreams. She studied under one of the best, John Paul Jackson. This book is a must-have for dreamers, their spouses, and even their children. You'll be amazed at how God uses ordinary circumstances to reveal special meaning. I highly recommend this book—hardly a day goes by without someone asking me about dreams. Kathy has done a remarkable job writing it."

Lisa Kratz Thomas
Speaker | Advocate | Author of
From the Crack House to the State House: Transforming Adversity
into Opportunity
Expertise in Substance Abuse Recovery
Prisoner Reentry
Life-Affirming Transformation

"The course of history has been dramatically shaped by dreams. The Bible details many of these events from Joseph, Pharaoh, Kings of Babylon and many, many more. God is speaking and we need to listen! Kathy loves dreams and she loves God who speaks through them. The joy to which she approaches God's dream language is beautifully contagious and extremely helpful. As an avid dreamer who has walked closely with the Lord since childhood, I've taken many classes and courses on understanding dreams. I thought I had a decent grasp on how God speaks in dreams, but Kathy's insights took my understanding to another level. Kathy is a passionate, gifted teacher with a wealth of knowledge gained through years of training that you will find inside the pages of *A New Lens*. Pick up this book, start learning, and let God speak to you through one of His favorite languages: dreams."

Philipa A. Booyens
Screenwriter "8 DAYS" and "I'm Not Ashamed"
Author of *Arise: You are Called to Be a Woman of Influence*
Creative director for After Eden Pictures and After Eden Talent

"If you feel a sense of apprehension or caution at the prospect of biblical dream interpretation, you're not alone. It's a bit unsettling to think that buried among those crazy and sometimes unsettling images that invade our sleep, our loving heavenly Father might actually have something He's trying to say to us! Well, it's about time someone took a detailed look at what the Bible has to say about dreams, and more importantly, what we can learn about ourselves and about Gods' character, nature and promises when we take a closer look at them. In my opinion, there is no one better to do it than my good friend, Kathy Gray. She is rooted and grounded in the truth of God's Word and has a God-given passion to share the tools God has equipped her with to bring insight and clarity to our dreams."

Neil Boron
Radio Talk Host
WDCX Radio, Buffalo, NY

"Kathy Gray has written a very personal and powerful invitation into one of the most overlooked, yet deeply spiritual aspects of the Christian life: our dreams. With decades of study and experience behind her, coupled with wisdom and a deep passion for the Holy Spirit, Kathy opens the door to a realm where God still speaks, heals, and guides through the night parables of dreams. Her voice is both seasoned and sincere, shaped by decades of experience and a passion to see others discover the richness of God's communication. She has been instrumental in my own life as it pertains to what God is speaking to me in the night watches. This book is not just informative, it's transformative. She has challenged me to pay attention, to lean in, and to believe that God truly desires to speak to His people in the quiet of the night. Whether you're a longtime dreamer or just beginning to wonder if your dreams might carry meaning, this book will stir your faith and increase your expectation. I believe it is a timely and vital tool for the Body of Christ in this hour. Prepare to be awakened—to your dreams and to the heart of God behind them."

Julie King
VP of Arise Movement
East-West

"In a generation that is burned out on religion and hungry for the supernatural, Kathy Gray is a seasoned equipper, practitioner, and Christ-formed leader who skillfully comes alongside to place our hands in the Hand of the Creator. Whether you are an avid dreamer of God's 'night parables' or seeking to understand someone in your life who is, *A New Lens* is a resource to awaken you to the power and beauty of God-given dreams, while grounding and instructing you in dream interpretation through a biblical lens. Jump in, shift perspective, and receive a new understanding of the voice of the Father to you in the night hours. God is *still speaking* through dreams and visions – it is time for the Western church to treasure the diamonds He is leaving under our pillows."

Pastor Roland Worton
Founder, Soundforgers and Lead Pastor, NEON Dallas
Author, *Emerging Worship* & *The Surprising Power of Joy*

A NEW LENS

Encountering God Through Dreams

KATHY GRAY

A New Lens
Encountering God Through Dreams
Kathy Gray

Contact the author:
Kathy@KathyGrayMinistries.org

Edited by:

Mary Ethel

Mary Ethel Eckard
Frisco, Texas

Library of Congress Control Number: 2025912128
ISBN (Print): 978-1-966561-16-3
ISBN (E-book): 978-1-966561-17-0

Dedication

This book is dedicated to the King of Kings,
the biggest Dreamer of all.
And to people everywhere who long to hear
from God through their dreams.

CONTENTS

ACKNOWLEDGMENTS

To my husband, Dave—for always believing in me and reminding me I can do it, for feeding me when I'm immersed in writing, for keeping me on track, for tackling endless details with the ministry, and for lending me your proof-reading eagle eye. Your hard work and steady presence give me the freedom to pursue learning and writing, and I'm forever grateful. You truly are the best guy.

To our four sons, Michael, Daniel, Jamison, and Bryan—for cheering me on and lending your fresh insights. For always making me feel welcome and cared for, soothing me with your music, and filling my life with more joy, color, and laughter than I ever thought possible.

To my sister, Karen—for being my kindred spirit in dreams since we were little, for your generous hospitality during countless visits, for being my personal chauffeur through the stunning Colorado mountains, and for patiently waiting to play Rummikub while I wrote (and wrote... and wrote).

To Ben and Nicole Rutledge—thank you for so generously sharing your incredible expertise to help bring my website and online presence to life. Colie, your momma was such a true encouragement in this ministry, and I know she would be so proud to see you excelling in stewarding dreams. I'm honored to have you both co-laboring in what God is doing.

To Mike and Amanda Wise—gifted teachers in dream interpretation and the ways of God—thank you for being an integral part of this journey even before we met personally. I'm deeply grateful for your rich friendship, your seasoned wisdom in dreams, and your unwavering encouragement in this ministry.

To John Paul Jackson—thank you for saying "yes" to the Lord and for revealing the powerful way you interpreted dreams through a biblical lens. I'm deeply grateful for your love and for your incredible service, the countless hours you spent writing and teaching, and for making this wisdom accessible and impactful for the rest of us.

To Hannah Birch and Ashley Watson—thank you for consistently showing up and selflessly sharing your wisdom on countless dream panels. Your dedication and service have been a tremendous gift. Your beautiful connection with the Holy Spirit and remarkable insights have made live dream interpretation an absolute joy.

To my dear friend and co-author of *Light In Our Darkness*, Lisa Kratz Thomas—thank you for always pushing me to do far more than I ever thought possible. You continue to encourage me beyond my comfort zone—whether I like it or not—and I'm better for it.

To my long-time kindred spirit, Lori Meyer, for telling me that dreams really do mean something, and for pointing me to John Paul Jackson. That simple nudge changed everything.

To Bonnie Hayes and Suzanna Nichols—your faithful friendship, prophetic words, and years of prayerful partnership have been a steady anchor for me. Thank you for seeing what I couldn't see on my own and for showing up to countless seminars and for opening doors for me to teach in multiple impactful environments.

To Michael Miller—thank you for your friendship, your willingness to teach our community about the gifts and power of the Holy Spirit, and for graciously agreeing to write the foreword. Thank you for ministering to my family in Colorado. I'm deeply grateful for your generosity in opening a space for me with your congregation and on "The Remnant Radio."

To our incredible Dream Community—thank you for your steady support throughout the development of all the seminars and this project. You took a risk to learn about dreams, and along the way, you've offered faithful friendship, brought clarity to my own dreams, and generously shared your experiences. Without you, this book would not have been written. I'm so grateful for each of you!

FOREWORD

In ancient Israel there was a debate between a man who had suffered beyond belief and his three friends. This sufferer believed he had been wronged by God and wanted his day in court so he could plead his case before God. Two of his friends, though I hesitate to call them that, are convinced this man is suffering deservedly because of his own sin, and they begin to argue with him at the foolish notion that God would speak with him. The author of Job has set the story up brilliantly and waited till the last moment for the truth teller and voice of reason, Job's youngest friend, to finally speak. Job 33:14 "Indeed, God does speak, here one way, and there another." He then goes on to talk about how God will speak in visions of the night, what we call dreams.

I have been a pastor for around fourteen years and have been teaching on the various ways God speaks for around twenty years. I have travelled all over the world speaking on this very topic. One thing that is common across the globe is that the Holy Spirit is still speaking just as He always has. I have also had dreams since I was a child. However, I have never been that good at interpreting them and have always relied on close friends or my wife to help me. Fortunately, God has always provided others who can help me explain what I had thought ineffable.

Kathy happens to be one of those especially gifted people, much like Joseph, to help in that very thing. I first met her when I was attending the Village Church. My family and I, at the time, were quite new to the church and came there in one of the more difficult seasons in our life. We had lost most of our friends and community and knew only one thing; we were moving back to Denver, Colorado to plant a church. We would only be in Dallas for one year. Despite that, Kathy was one of the first people at the Village Church who welcomed us into the community and introduced us to many who became long-lasting friends. These were also the friends that would send us back to Denver with resources and their prayer support.

Coincidentally, the year we planted our church in Denver, Colorado was 2020. We met as a community for three weeks before COVID shut us down and forced this tiny community to stop before we started. During this time, Kathy and the others from the Village Community were a lifeline of prayer support and more. We had no idea how Kathy, in particular, would provide resources beyond what we could have ever dreamed, pun very much intended. My wife and I had a three-year-old boy and a one-year-old daughter when suddenly the grocery stores sold out of wet wipes and toilet paper. We were desperate.

Little did we know that Kathy had been stocking up on toilet paper and wet wipes for the last couple of years, likely causing no small amount of curiosity from her husband and others who knew about it. Why had she been stocking up on toilet paper and wet wipes? God had given her a dream, and He had my wife and me in mind. Before disaster struck, I walked out of the house one day to find a giant package on my front porch with exactly what we needed.

I wonder how many other ways God has used dreams like these to bring provision and encouragement to others in the midst of their distress. What if Kathy had just ignored the dream, not stocked up on toilet paper because she had interpreted the dream to be only symbolic and not instructive? Fortunately for the Miller family, Kathy knew what to do with her dreams and knows how to help others understand the various ways God is speaking to them, as well, which is why a book like this is needed. If God speaks to us in matters small, like what I have described, and cares even about the little things, then how much more so the weightier matters?

In this book you will gain insights into the various ways God speaks and practical instructions to help ensure that you are not brushing off what might be vital instructions on what God might be saying to you. Kathy will share practical and biblical insights into how to capture and make the most of what God is communicating. She will answer questions like, how do I know if something is a warning in a dream or a foretelling of what will certainly come to pass? Is this dream literal or are there symbols meant to be interpreted? Is the dream about me or those around me and how do I know the difference?

This book is an invitation to friendship with God. Jesus said to his disciples in John 15:15, *"I have called you friends for everything I hear from my Father I make known to you."* The essence of fellowship is knowing and being fully known. It is not obligatory but comes through the simple joy of being with someone you love. I believe the biblical content found here will help bring you one step closer to a deeper friendship with Jesus.

Michael Miller
Cohost of The Remnant Radio
Elder at Reclamation Church in Denver, Colorado

INTRODUCTION

*"God is literally leaving diamonds under our pillows at night,
and we are throwing them away."*
~ Matt Lockett, Justice House of Prayer DC

The pages to follow hold an invitation to embark on an adventure—one that explores a virtually untapped realm. A realm filled with hidden treasures just waiting to be unearthed. Our dreams. The landscape of this dimension is as varied and distinct as the person journeying through it. And every man, woman, and child *does* venture into this realm—some infrequently, while others find themselves there every time they close their eyes. The question is: How should we respond to the visions and experiences we bring back from our dreams?

I'm convinced that now, more than ever, we urgently need the skill of interpreting dreams through a biblical lens. Yet, for a number of reasons, the practice of stewarding these often mysterious and perplexing experiences has largely been lost in the Western church—if dreams are even considered at all.

Few can deny the profound changes that have occurred globally since 2020. We've all been affected in one way or another, and many are now seeking to understand God's mind during these shifts. In this season we truly need to gain His kingdom perspective to navigate these accelerated times of change. The good news is that we have an often-overlooked treasure trove of wisdom, guidance, and revelation right at our fingertips! This gold mine is nothing new, and it's not New

Age. Dreams and their interpretation were God's idea from the very beginning!

Since I was young, I've loved Jesus and studied His Word, and from my earliest memories, I've always been a dreamer. However, it wasn't until my 30s that I realized how deeply intertwined valuing dreams and walking with Jesus truly are. Learning the art of partnering with the Holy Spirit to process these experiences unlocked a completely new dimension of joy in my life! Tuning in to God's "night parables" has expanded my understanding of His character beyond anything I expected—and it's drawn me into a deeper love for both the Lord and others. This is not an either/or reality – it's both/and. It involves both the ongoing study and application of God's Word, and a willingness to engage with all forms of His communication as demonstrated throughout Scripture.

Over time, I've come to realize that a "new lens" is vital for the Body of Christ to more fully recognize and receive the ways the Lord speaks through dreams—it's a key part of growing in intimacy with Him. A lens of seeing the value of dreams and tools to interpret them accurately through a biblical worldview. James 1:5 encourages us to ask for wisdom, and God guarantees that He will give it generously. I would imagine that, like me, you've taken Him up on this promise and asked for wisdom yourself. What if the answer to our search is already being released, but it's coming to us in one of God's preferred ways of communicating — packaged in a dream?

Having experienced the riches of dream interpretation through a biblical lens, my heart longs to see sons and daughters of God join with the Holy Spirit to rediscover the powerful realm of dreams in their own lives! I long for the day when men, women, and children go to bed each night with hearts full of expectation, ready to hear from the Lord as they sleep.

This book is the fruit of more than two decades of studying dream interpretation through the lens of Scripture, coupled with eight years of teaching these principles to others. What follows is not an in-depth theological analysis or a debate on whether God still speaks through dreams and visions. Rather, it is an invitation to deepen your connection with the Lord through your dreams and the dreams of those around you.

In each chapter, we'll delve into real dreams and examine the profound impact they have had on the lives of those who received them. Dreams are not just a function of our brain or imagination – they are genuine spiritual encounters. They take place in a realm unseen by most of us, yet in a dimension that is often more substantial than what we perceive in the natural world through our five senses. Come to think of it, perhaps that's why the Scriptures are filled with dreams and visions, demonstrating just how much the unseen realm affects what happens in the physical world.

My sincere prayer is that what you find here will spark hope in your spirit. That as you engage with the Holy Spirit about your dreams, you would receive fresh insight, revelation, and encouragement. God is on the move. He is stirring His people worldwide, inviting us to experience the depth of His multifaceted Presence through the many ways He speaks to us.

I foresee a company of believers, equipped and dependent on the Holy Spirit, helping people in all spheres of life to interpret their dreams and to encounter the heart of God. I'm anticipating deeper revelation of the heavenly wisdom the Father is imparting through dreams—wisdom that will transform our families, communities, nations, and the world.

May the Spirit of Jesus awaken and empower you as you read on!

"May God himself, the God who makes everything holy and whole, make you holy and whole, put you together – spirit, soul, and body – and keep you fit for the coming of our Master, Jesus Christ. The One who called you is completely dependable. If He said it, He'll do it!"
~ 1 Thessalonians 5:23 MSG

Chapter 1

WHY DREAMS?

Enjoying a cool spring evening out on his back porch, one of my sons and I were engaged in an impassioned conversation. We often have differing perspectives on issues, and I relish these times of discussion. Back and forth, we talk through matters of the heart, problems in society, and world perspectives. There is no win or lose in these exchanges. He brings viewpoints I haven't considered, and I do the same for him. This particular evening, question after challenging question came my direction as he probed the validity of the biblical dream interpretation courses I was attending and the integrity of the ministry teaching them.

"Aren't those people televangelists?"

"How do they make their money?"

"Do they actually charge for those conferences?"

I responded with a question: *"Let me ask you this. If one of your favorite authors, who happens to be a Christian, writes a book, do you think they should charge for it?"*

"Of course!" was his immediate reply.

"So, tell me," I continued, *"if you developed a 250-page curriculum, paid for the venue, hosted a seminar, and taught for 3 days, do you think you would charge for it?"*

He smiled in understanding. *"Well, yes,"* he responded.

There was an easy break in the conversation as we savored the evening colors and breathed in the cool breeze. I was wondering why his sudden vetting of the ministry that was teaching biblical dream interpretation. With his next question his reasons came to light.

Turning to me with an earnest expression, he asked, *"Mom, is Dad mad at me? I've been having lots of dreams where Dad is angry with me and disappointed. Is he upset with me?"*

I paused for a moment, considering his dreams. Of course, my momma's heart hurt that he was even thinking along those lines. I asked him a question in return. *"Hon, tell me something. Do you kind of feel like God is disappointed with you? That you aren't measuring up?"*

"Oh yeah, all the time," he admitted matter-of-factly.

I nodded in understanding. I reassured him that no, his dad wasn't upset with him. On the contrary, his dad was incredibly proud of him, admired him, and treasured the time he spent with him!

"I believe those dreams are God trying to show you how you view your Heavenly Father, and how you believe He sees you."

Relief registered on his face.

I went on, *"Here's the reality. The Heavenly Father isn't like that at all. You could never earn His approval - you already have it. You have it because of Jesus. He isn't mad at you, or even disappointed in you. He knew what He was getting when He made you, when He died for you. He loves you now, just as you are, and not a future version of yourself. I believe these dreams are an invitation to let go of a distorted view of the Father and choose to embrace His perfect love for you!"*

In that moment, I was truly grateful for the teaching and training I'd received in dream interpretation through a biblical lens. Sharing and reasoning through dreams has proved to be an incredible launching pad for building deeper connections with one another. That encounter with my son, and with hundreds like it with others, is just one of the reasons I'm grateful that God speaks through dreams. He's pursuing us with His love even while we sleep.

I can tell you, though, that even the *idea* that God pursues us in love through dreams never once crossed my mind until I was well into my 30s. Isn't it remarkable how we can pursue knowing God for years and yet *completely* miss a significant truth? A truth that profoundly affects everyday life. Just not connecting the dots?

For me, despite dreams and visions filling the pages from Genesis to Revelation, I never saw them as relevant to my own life. More ironic still, I missed this truth even though I had been a lifelong, nightly vivid dreamer. Since childhood, as I wake up every morning, I am conscious of at least one and usually multiple dreams.

These days, I welcome dreams as what they truly are - a gift. However, far into my early adult years, I viewed dreams as anything *but* a gift. To be honest, I would have called them some sort of curse in my life. That is if I ever talked about them at all, which I rarely did. In my mind, if I never dreamed again, I would have been ok with that. I'm so glad that God often doesn't give us what we think we want.

I had a pretty good reason for my adversarial relationship with dreams. Night after night, I would be jolted awake from intense and terrifying nightmares, or my eyes would fly open only to see some ghoulish manifestation in my darkened bedroom. Not my idea of a good time!

There were nights when I would have some thrilling dream, like flying effortlessly over a beautiful moonlit landscape. However, more often than not, I would wake up yelling, gripped by terror from the dreams, or screaming at whatever figure or creature I could see in my bedroom. Suffice it to say, sleep and I were not on friendly terms.

Other than my sister (did you know dreaming often runs in families?), I simply didn't know anyone else "like me." I didn't talk about these "strange" nighttime experiences with my friends because, well, frankly, it was embarrassing. A sense of being alone in this experience of dreams overwhelmed me. Quality of sleep wasn't something I seemed to have any control over. I would sleep and I would be tormented. Today I know that a major strategy of the enemy of our souls is to intimidate or terrify children to keep them from hearing from God in their dreams. (More on children and dreams in Chapter 13.)

In our extended family of dreamers, the dreams were attributed to a "vivid imagination." The dark spiritual encounters? "Hallucinations." What else could they be? In our Bible-rich, devout ministry environment, there was no biblical teaching on dreams or their significance. And this is still true in many segments of the Body of Christ today.

Don't misunderstand me—our family was deeply immersed in a vivacious Christian life. I was raised in an atmosphere saturated with the sounds of music and the warmth of laughter. Our lives were rich with activity, a supportive community of believers, memorable vacations, and the beauty of Colorado that surrounded us. Our vibrant family life is one reason those distressing dreams felt so disconnected from our everyday reality.

It never occurred to me that there was an upside to dreaming, and in my child's mind, when I thought about it, I was convinced something was seriously wrong with me. And I was exhausted. All the time. I attributed this to a character issue. I must be lazy.

This cycle of nightmares and unsettling encounters continued throughout my college years and, like an unwelcome squatter, followed me into marriage and motherhood. But everything changed in my late twenties with a single conversation.

Have you ever had an encounter where an unexpected response triggered a shift that altered your trajectory? Ever received unexpected understanding and grace?

On a quiet Colorado afternoon while my little boys were napping, I sat sipping coffee with a dear family friend. Pricilla is a tall, elegant Southern woman with a resonant voice and a soothing drawl. She radiates beauty and dignity. Seated across my dining room table, she earnestly asked about my well-being. My brother had recently been tragically killed in a crime of violence, and it had shaken me to the core.

Pricilla had reached out to see how I was navigating this devastating loss. Our conversation was unhurried and comfortable. Her warmth and direct manner put me at ease.

"So, how are y'all really doin', Kathy?"

Somehow, her presence created an authentic atmosphere free of judgment, and I was surprised to hear myself confiding in her about the inexplicable nightmares and bizarre appearances in the night. I told her how exhausted I felt most of the time.

She took a moment before responding and then spoke these words that shifted the course of my life.

"Honey, that's not normal. And you don't have to live that way."

Stunned silence. I certainly did not see that coming! I had braced myself for a blank stare, a pitying look, or a weak, "I'll pray for you," followed by a hasty retreat. Pricilla's response, *"...and you don't have to live that way,"* instantly produced a paradigm shift within me. Hope. Hope that something better was possible flooded my soul.

She went on, *"I have a friend who I think can help you."*

Over the course of the next year, I met with this friend-turned-mentor who prayed and listened to the Holy Spirit with me. Amazingly, the nightmares stopped as years of buried, undealt-with pain made its way out of the dark and into the light of day.

I came to understand that recurring nightmares can be a red flag for unresolved trauma—pain that the Father longs to heal with His love and power. Healing began to take root in my troubled soul, and the nightmares dissipated as I brought hidden realities into the light. He really does turn our sorrow into joy and gives us beauty for ashes. [1]

Now that I was free from nightmares, I thought I'd be finished with dreams. Good riddance! I'd finally be "normal." Much to my surprise, the beauty that unfolded for me was not a dreamless life. I dreamt just as much as before. These dreams, even if I didn't understand them, were filled with riddles, meaning, and revelation. I didn't know it then, but just around the corner, I would be entering a life-changing pursuit of God in ways I had never imagined. Ways that were already lying in the pages of Scripture, hiding in plain sight.

REFLECTIONS

1. How has your perspective on dreams changed over time? Can you relate to the author's initial fear and confusion about dreams?

   _____

   _____

   _____

2. Have you ever experienced a shift in your thinking after someone shared an unexpected perspective with you?

   _____

   _____

   _____

3. How do you currently view the role of dreams in your life?

   _____

   _____

   _____

4. Are there any patterns in your family that influence how you view dreams?

_____

_____

_____

5. Are you open to the idea that God can speak to you through your dreams?

_____

_____

_____

Chapter 2

CHANGING THE FILTER

Dream:

> "*I entered a garden behind an enormous house (I knew it was heaven) and saw The Father sitting in a rocking chair watching all His children enjoy a party in the garden. He was smiling so big. The exaggerated feature was the large smile wrinkles on The Father's face. From above His eyes, all the way down His chin, He had smile wrinkles. They opened His face like a curtain, and I knew He was pleased.*
>
> "*What made this feature so important was an earlier scene with an earthly father. The dad was sitting in a dark, shrouded corner, hunched over and angry. Above him was the name "Cannot Be Pleased." Several scenes later, here was The Father who was completely pleased. The smile wrinkles were so deep and large and comforting.*
>
> "*When I woke up, I was comforted that I had the freedom to let go of some past hurts and trust God's love and plan. I can't describe it without my eyes getting teary because it was so happy, and I knew none of His children's worries could take*

away His pleasure and satisfaction. The joy and affection felt permanent." – *C.T.*

It was a late Saturday afternoon in the Spring of 2003. In a beautiful little church somewhere in Dallas, I sat riveted, listening to one of the biblical dream interpretation teachers. I didn't know anyone else in the seminar that day, so I was sitting by myself in a pew halfway back in the sanctuary. I had a burning hunger to learn about dreams, visions, etc., and I would drive any distance to get my hands on all the teaching I could.

These topics weren't exactly popular topics in the Bible church we were attending. We were in a busy season of life, but this hunger for *more* compelled me to travel all over the Dallas - Fort Worth metroplex to attend workshops and conferences.

That particular day, as I sat through the seminar, I wrote copious notes in the handouts we were given. The pages were littered with question marks circled emphatically. I underlined and drew arrows to sections detailing concepts that were unfamiliar and puzzling to me. My critical thoughts flew onto the handouts.

*"How did they get **that** from that passage?"*

"I've never heard that before - pretty sure that's not right."

"Wait a minute, I've been told that's 'unbiblical.'"

"I'll have to look that word up in the Strong's Concordance."

"Didn't some council in the 4th century decide against that?"

"Do they have any verifiable evidence this is still true for today?"

From the mental gymnastics tumbling through my head, you might be wondering why I even attended. But that's the thing about a burning in your bones, fanned by the Holy Spirit. You can't ignore it, no matter how much you're kicking and screaming inside. The truth is, I was genuinely desperate to learn and practice the works of Jesus. I literally ached for that to be a reality in my life. I just didn't know how.

But one thing was sure - I was not going to be taken for a fool. I knew that I needed to *"study to show myself approved...rightly dividing the word of truth.*[2] I was determined I wouldn't be taken in by "false teaching." So, naturally, I filtered everything through *my* best understanding of the Scriptures and life. Looking back, I would ask my 20-year younger self, "So how's that working for you?"

Oh, I was *genuinely* asking God for breakthrough and understanding. I was willing and putting in the effort. But it wasn't coming very easily. Ok, it was more like slogging through sludge on a foggy day. In spite of my sincere desire, I had a problem. A big one. This problem was profoundly hindering me from receiving truths with an understanding heart. And that problem, friends, was *ME*. I just couldn't see it.

I walked out of the seminar into a fresh, beautiful, rain-kissed, sunny afternoon. Vibrant, shimmering colors covered the landscape. My mind, however, was anything but fresh and sunny as I wrestled and prayed over the concepts taught that day. Well, sort of praying, but honestly, mostly just mentally battling. I really wanted all of this, but I was conflicted.

I started my car and settled in for the long drive home. A few minutes later, I was crossing over a bridge and, with unmistakable clarity in my spirit, I heard the Holy Spirit giving me a piece of advice. A golden piece of advice that would change my life.

"Why don't you just take it all in and let ME be your filter?"

Wait, let the Holy Spirit be my filter? What a concept. Actually, what a *biblical* concept.

Up until that time, I had firmly believed that *I* was responsible for being my *own* filter. That my best understanding would keep me from being led astray. That I needed to avoid listening to, or even considering, what *might possibly* be "false teaching."

With those few words, *"Just take it all in and let Me be your filter,"* a huge weight of anxiety lifted from my heart. The Lord knew my deep desire was to discover and submit to His ways in all areas of my life. In His perfect wisdom, He could see what a stumbling block my current filter was.

My response was an immediate, *"Yes, Sir."*

What incredible freedom this revelation brought me. I could rest and receive and let the *Lord* be my discernment. After all, I realized, He *is* the Wonderful Counselor. I could trust Him to keep me from falling into deception. Even better, I could trust Him to lead me *out* of deception when heading in the wrong direction.

Psalm 23 rang in my spirit,

> *"You lead me in paths of righteousness for Your name's sake.*
> *Your rod (gentle course correction) and staff (pulling me from danger),*
> *they comfort me."*

What a change in perspective. In fact, the truth is that every one of us sees the world through a filter. It's impossible not to, and it's a good thing. God has placed us in exactly the right geographical spot and in the exact bloodline He purposed so that we would find Him and live out His destiny for us (Acts 17:26).[3] Because of this, our experiences in our culture, our personality, our upbringing, teaching we've received, our hurts and successes, even the dominant mindset of our region – all inform our "filter." Just like the dream at the beginning of this chapter, the dreamer's lens shifted as the Heavenly Father revealed His true delight in her and joyful nature.

When I gave the reins of my filter over to the Holy Spirit, I experienced a genuine lens change. Reading, studying, and memorizing Scripture, along with sitting under solid biblical teaching remained the primary focus. Accountability with mature believers never faded from the rhythm of life. But I began experiencing an acceleration in understanding as never before. Like a "seeing eye picture," when I relaxed and focused, I could finally perceive the hidden images that were there all along.

A deep hunger filled me to understand and become proficient in discerning God's communication in dreams through a biblical lens. From then on, I dedicated myself to understanding how God communicates through *all* the ways He reveals Himself in Scripture. By this time, my husband, Dave, and I were juggling four boys, I was teaching piano, and he worked full time and traveled. We both saw the need to grow in these things, and he held down the fort while I attended multiple three-day conferences with John Paul Jackson at Streams Ministries.[4]

These teaching sessions were packed with biblical instruction on the multi-faceted character of God, highlighting the need for our character to align with His. Scripture after Scripture was unpacked in ways I had never seen. I found that I was no longer alone in my pursuit of all the ways of God. Dave and I, along with some of our community, attended monthly evening sessions where John Paul Jackson covered biblical topics not normally (or ever) addressed on Sunday mornings, at retreats, or during weekly Bible studies.

I began journaling my dreams and dialogued with the Holy Spirit to understand their meaning. And I practiced. My sister, Karen, also a prolific dreamer, and I would get on the phone and analyze our dreams together, praying for insight. I began receiving dreams that involved our church, where a group of us served as intercessors. Dreams that offered encouragement, revealed what God was about to do, provided prayer strategies, or gave warnings.

I spoke frequently with those within and outside the church about the importance of dreams. Those I encountered throughout the week seemed genuinely interested and shared some of their dreams. My close friends understood that our dreams carried messages, and we helped each other interpret them. Within the Christian community, however, while a few people were open to the idea, most responded with blank stares, quickly changed the subject, dismissed it condescendingly, or subtly warned me about the dangers of dream interpretation, urging me to focus solely on the Bible.

Regardless of what kind of response I received, I knew that God had *redeemed* a huge area of my life, and I was excited about it! Dreams and endeavoring to interpret them with the Holy Spirit was producing consistently good fruit in my life. I was receiving God's wisdom on circumstances that troubled me, correction on unfruitful patterns, warnings about unhealthy relationships, counsel for parenting, encouraging encounters with God – all from dreams. And I knew I wasn't the only one—others were having dreams and visions too, even if they weren't discussing them openly.

One December evening in 2016, our home was filled to capacity for our annual Christmas piano recital. After the performance, relieved little musicians were darting in and out of the kitchen, loading up their plates with hors d'oeuvres and grabbing refills of Christmas punch. While parents mingled and chatted, I was catching up with one of the moms, my friend Rachel Joy, the founder of a pioneering ministry dedicated to empowering women and communities through dignified and sustainable employment opportunities.[5] Rachel values how God communicates through dreams, and we had often discussed her dreams, along with a few of mine that I felt were specifically meant for her and her ministry.

As we chatted over the sound of happy voices and Christmas music in the background, she asked if I'd be willing to teach a group of women she was mentoring about dreams and visions. I took about half a second to think it over, then blurted out, "Yes, I'd love to!"

And so began my journey of developing seminars to pass along what had so radically changed my life!

REFLECTIONS

1. When faced with new or unfamiliar teachings, how do you typically respond? Do you approach them with curiosity or with skepticism, like the author did in the seminar?

_____

_____

_____

2. Can you recall a time when your initial interpretation of something turned out to be incorrect? How did your perspective shift once you allowed yourself to be open to a new understanding?

_____

_____

_____

3. What role might fear play in your approach to learning and spiritual growth? How might fear of being deceived or misunderstood affect your ability to receive truths that are new to you?

_____

_____

_____

4. Do you trust the Holy Spirit to guide you and filter the information you encounter? What might it look like for you to relinquish control and allow God to be your filter?

_____

_____

_____

5. How do your past experiences, upbringing, or cultural background shape the way you interpret biblical teachings and dreams? Are there areas where your personal filter needs to be adjusted or renewed?

_____

_____

_____

Chapter 3

WHAT HAPPENED TO DREAMS IN THE CHURCH?

*"There is a realm of the Spirit that we can walk in that the New Age craves. And the reason why they're not in church is **not** because they don't crave God, it's because they've found the church **unresponsive to their experience.**"*
~ John Paul Jackson

Years ago, we drove a few hours for a weekend getaway with our friends, Mark and Jean, at their beautiful lake house. Their grown children had joined us, which included their son and his lovely new wife. As the sun was setting that first evening, we all gathered around the long, rustic dinner table for a meal. As soon as the meal was blessed, our friend, Mark, turned to me and said, *"So, Kathy, I hear you interpret dreams."* I would say I froze with my fork halfway to my mouth, but we hadn't even passed the food.

Caught off guard by that unexpected conversation opener, I stammered something like, "Uh, well yes... I mean as best I know how." With that, the dreams started coming one right after another. Jolted out of "vacation brain," my focus kicked into high gear. I listened and pictured each dream in my spirit. I asked lots of clarifying questions. Mostly, though, I was inwardly shooting up eloquent prayers such as, "Help!"

Despite my internal panic, the dreams were fascinating, and the conversation dynamic. Around the table, everyone got involved as we worked through them together. After the interpretations of several dreams had been illuminated, their new daughter-in-law nudged her husband, "Tell the dream you've had so many times."

He launched into describing the dream:

> *"I've had this dream anywhere from 15-25 times. I can remember having this dream as early as age 3-4 and as recent as within the last 2-3 years. Although the dream varies slightly each time I have it, there are a few constants.*
>
> *"The dream starts differently each time, but a typical version starts with me playing in our backyard at our childhood house in Virginia. I am my present age; it is never a flashback, and I'm always by myself. The backyard backs up to very thick woods, but we had a single dogwood tree that was right on the edge of the yard and where the woods begin. The tree is very distinct. It is a young dogwood with white leaves/petals, but it willows over and is nearly touching the ground from where I can see it.*
>
> *"I usually lose a ball, or for some other reason, I'm drawn to the tree. Once I get to the tree, I pull back the branches in search of whatever I've lost, and there are three black snakes there. The snakes are so intertwined together that they look like a bowl of noodle soup.*
>
> *"As I watch the snakes continue to do their thing, I notice stripes on the snakes from head to toe. Each snake has a different color; one yellow, one blue, and one red. One of the snakes always stands out more than the other. I'm not sure*

how, but I just know that one is more distinct than the rest. Every time I have the dream, the one that is distinct changes.

"For some reason, I always try to reach around the pile of snakes, or sometimes I'm standing, and I step over them. (I think it's so that I can get whatever I have lost. Each time I have the dream, whatever I'm looking for is different.) When I do try to get over them, one of them bites me, and I wake up.

"Sometimes, though, there is a rock under the tree. When I move the rock, I find the snakes. When I do have the rock, I'm able to smash the snakes, and when I smash the snakes, I wake up."

What an incredible dream; so profound, it astonished me.

I asked a few clarifying questions such as, "Were the colors vivid?" and "Was anyone else there?" Again, my spirit continued inwardly having a steady stream of dialogue with the Holy Spirit.

Although there are aspects in the dream I won't address here, this is basically how I responded with what I believed to be the interpretation.

"I believe the dream is from the Lord, and it's about your life. The three snakes represent lies with which the enemy is trying to negatively affect you. Those lies come packaged in fear, depression or anger. Each time you have this dream, the Lord is highlighting which of those three applies to your current situation. The dream is letting you in on a secret - the enemy's playbook, so to speak. Whenever you see fear or depression or anger crop up in you, especially in seasons of searching, you can know there is a lie attached to it. If you try to avoid dealing with the lie, it'll 'bite you' or negatively impact you. On the other hand, if you crush it with the Rock, (Jesus - your authority in Christ, the mind of Christ in you), you'll defeat it and be free of the lie."

"That's exactly what happens to him!" several of the family members said at the same time. We were all amazed how the dream illustrated the patterns he experiences in his life with such detailed accuracy. Even more remarkable was that the dream offered a solution to the tough situations he would encounter.

I didn't know the specifics of his challenges, but God did, and the dream addressed them directly. I was once again amazed by the meticulous care of a loving Father who would craft a dream so specific to the dreamer and bring it back at just the right moments in his life. The color on the snake was like an "X marks the spot – dig here" to help him discover and take authority over a lie of the enemy.

His story is just one of hundreds I've come across. The Body of Christ is in desperate need of dream interpreters who hold a biblical worldview. The Lord hasn't stopped releasing dreams just because we haven't fully recognized their significance. We're just as much in need of guidance as the despairing fellow inmates of Joseph in Egypt.

*"So Joseph asked Pharaoh's officers who were with him in the custody of his lord's house, saying, 'Why do you look so sad today?' And they said to him, 'We each have had a dream, **and there is no interpreter of it.'"***
~ Genesis 40:7, 8

The church community where I began teaching dream interpretation believed that all of the gifts of the Spirit were for today, but they had yet to build out structures to train people in those gifts. Our lead pastor was fully on board and eager for the whole church to operate in every gift. From time to time, he would connect me with individuals who were trying to make sense of their experiences and giftings. Another way of saying that is he sent the "weird" folks my way. Birds of a feather and all.

On one such occasion, he connected me with a young woman who had just walked away from New Age practices. She had grown up loving Jesus but felt out of place in the church because she had so many experiences that no one seemed to understand or validate. Unable to ignore the spiritual realities she was encountering and lacking any discipleship —or even encouragement — in the evangelical community, she eventually found herself fully immersed in New Age practices. At least there, everyone seemed to understand her.

The problem with New Age is this: although New Age, Eastern religions, and many other practices heartily embrace spiritual experiences, they operate in power energized by dark forces - by demons.[6] The goal of these experiences is control over their own lives, others, and the environment. Although intriguing and exhilarating, these encounters are unclean, and they defile those practicing them. Those atmospheres draw their followers away from the Light of God, deceiving them and leaving them empty.

> *"And our fellowship is with the Father and with his Son, Jesus Christ...This is the message we have heard from him and declare to you: God is light; in him there is no darkness at all."*
> ~ 1 John 1:4,5

My lovely new friend had re-surrendered her life to Jesus and was full of questions. How could she live out these giftings God had given her in a clean, life-giving way that is in harmony with the scripture? We had a rich time uncovering numerous biblical examples that reflected the very experiences she encountered while also reflecting on how God used those abilities to expand His Kingdom influence.

Having strayed so far from truth, it was evident she was fearful of "getting it wrong" again. Understandable. But any fear-driven approach will crowd out godly discernment. Fear of "being deceived" is the voice of an orphan, one who has yet to understand that they are fathered by the *best* Papa; an ever-watchful, faithful Shepherd. If we allow ourselves to steep in His all-encompassing, perfect love, fear is driven out[7] and we are positioned to receive His wisdom. Our

Any approach that is fear-driven will crowd out godly discernment.

21

Father has given us the unsurpassed Counselor who will lead and guide us into all truth.[8]

As I shared the biblical truths behind this paradigm shift, tears of relief and healing welled up in her eyes. She is currently pursuing understanding the ways of God in all areas of her life and has never again strayed into New Age practices.

A few years back when my beautiful cousin started awakening to the significance of dreams, she began sharing the dreams and visions she was experiencing. As she did so, she kept referring to manifestations from the unseen realm that she would see at night as "hallucinations." This didn't surprise me, as it was the only terminology I had known before I began studying these experiences in the Bible. A sudden idea sparked, prompting me to ask her a few questions that might help her better understand what she was really experiencing.

"Tell me," I began, *"do you drink heavily before bed?"* (I was well aware she didn't drink at all.)

"No!" she responded, sounding surprised that I would ask.

"Are you addicted to drugs?"

Again, a resounding, *"No, of course not!"*

I continued, *"How about medications? Are you heavily medicated?"*

A softer *"No..."* as she began to follow the direction of my thoughts.

With a final question, *"Have you been diagnosed with a mental illness?"* She laughed and responded, *"No."*

"Then you are not hallucinating! You are seeing in the supernatural realm."

So, how did we get to a point where the majority of devoted Christians have no training in or understanding of the "mystical" ways of God? Why do believers have to hunt to find the "weird ones" to help them out? What happened to a biblical comprehension of dreams, visions, and spiritual encounters in the Western church at large?

In much of our postmodern Western church culture, we have become accustomed to a certain set of priorities. We have valued intellect over revelation, substituted knowledge of Scripture for knowledge of the ways of God, exchanged Holy Spirit-filled encounters we "can't control" for planned-to-the-minute spectator-oriented meetings and conferences. Regrettably, we have mocked or feared experiences and practices we don't understand, opting to reject them completely. We have preached against biblical God-given gifts, constructing theologies that intimidate the listener from even investigating on their own. We teach our children to follow Jesus but neglect to train them to hear His voice.

Bottom line, many of us have lowered the acceptable truth about God and His ways to *our* level of experience, what we've been taught, or what we can rationally understand. We tend to downplay or reframe the unseen realm as something less mystical, even though the Bible consistently illustrates its active role and importance. I can say all of this with great certainty and without judgment. That is exactly what I did.

> Thankfully, the Holy Spirit, through the very Scriptures themselves, opened my understanding to the many ways God releases revelation.

Many of us don't even know we can be on the lookout for revelation. The only way I expected God to speak to me was through the Word. Most decisions felt like a guessing game. I couldn't find a scripture that told me what courses to enroll in, what job to take, or where I should go on vacation. I didn't have confidence that I could hear God's voice – I had never truly taken Jesus' promise in John 10:27 to heart.

"My sheep hear my voice, I know them, and they follow Me."
~ John 10:27

Thankfully, the Holy Spirit, through the very Scriptures themselves, opened my understanding to the many ways God releases revelation.

A few years back I attended a conference focused on merging "Word and Spirit" and was struck by a statement from one of the speakers: *"We might hear more from God if we quit insisting that He speak to us in the ways we prefer."*

As I grew in understanding the ways God communicates and began teaching about dreams, I started formulating questions as to why our culture has, by and large, set aside the more "mystical" ways of God.

- Why *is* it that we prefer linear answers that satisfy our logic?
- Why *do* we insist on hearing God's direction only through written Scripture, or a teacher we trust?
- Why is it so difficult to adopt metaphorical processing?
- Why, in all the seminars I've taught, have so few believers ever received biblical teaching on interpreting and stewarding dreams and their role in our lives and communities? (Let alone heard a message from the pulpit.)

I've come to understand several reasons why dreams, visions, and encounters are often dismissed or met with skepticism.

To begin with, much of it comes from Western vs. Eastern perspectives. The Bible was written by Easterners to Eastern people. Their way of processing information and seeing the world is very different from ours. It is a contrast of Greek culture (our major influence) versus Hebrew culture (the language of the Bible).

For instance, Greek-thinkers express truth through definitions and ideas. Hebrew-thinkers express truth with word pictures and stories. We like a well-organized outline, clear bullet points and actionable steps. Hebrews communicate in imagery, poetry, and symbolism. While the Greek perspective prioritizes analyzing and assessing information, the Hebrew mindset focuses on understanding through relationship.

A simple way to break this down is that the Greek approach leans heavily on left-brain qualities—logic, facts, and quantitative proof— while the Hebrew approach relies more on right-brain functions, like creativity, intuition, story, and metaphorical thinking.

An analogy I recently heard on a podcast humorously highlighted this difference in perspective. A Westerner and an Easterner walk into a laboratory and observe a dissected frog. The Westerner comments on the exposed ligaments, organs, and other physical characteristics of the unfortunate amphibian. The Easterner, on the other hand, asks, "Did he have a girlfriend? What was his family like?" In other words, how did he get here? What's the story behind what I'm observing right now?

Let's take numbers, for example. Numbers are straight-forward and concrete, right? To us Greek-thinkers, numbers primarily represent quantity. But to the Hebrew, numbers are multi-faceted, including quality and symbolism. So much so, their numbers are pictorial using images that express various concepts.

When the Greek-influenced culture considers God, the focus is on proving His existence and defining His nature. The Hebrew assumes the existence of God and focuses on the relationship, how He relates. For us, faith is based on creeds, belief statements and proof texting to support those beliefs. For the Hebrew, faith is relational and relies on experiences of and with God – both in Scripture, history, and personally.

The Greek mindset is focused on individual behavior and responsibility. Hebrew thinkers focus on community. In fact, much of the Epistles are directed toward "you" as a group. Or as we say in Texas, "All y'all" – together. How many of us have assumed that when Paul or other New Testament writers say, "you," they meant "me individually"? You may already know they are addressing whole communities or the Body of Christ at large, but our culture pulls on us to think it's about "me."

Western vs. Eastern Worldview	
Western / Greek Culture	Eastern / Hebrew Culture
Express truth through definitions and ideas	Express truth with word-pictures and stories
Prefer outlines, bullet points and application actions	Employs imagery, poetry, and symbolism
Focus is on evaluating information	Focus is on relationship
Numbers primarily represent quantity	Numbers are multi-faceted including quality and symbolism
Non-pictorial numbers	Numbers are pictorial, representing concepts
Focus is on proving God's existence	Assumes the existence of God
Focus is on defining God's nature	Focus is on the relationship, how He relates
Faith based on creeds, belief statements, and proof texting to support those beliefs	Faith is relational and relies on experiences of and with God – in Scripture, history and personally
Focus is on individual behavior and responsibility	Focus is on community – "all y'all"

Another reason I believe there is a huge gap of understanding dreams in our Western church culture is very simple. The enemy has successfully stolen / hidden this supernatural connection to heaven's realm. Through deception and missing information, we've been convinced we don't need to hear God's communication though dreams and visions. Our ears have been deafened and our eyes blinded to this profound language of our Creator. Some have even been hoodwinked into believing that evaluating dreams is demonic!

One final paradigm shift I believe is significant from a Western perspective to a biblical view is our concept of the 24-hour day. In our culture, we view the day as beginning in the morning when we wake up. "Up and at 'em!" In the Jewish culture, the "day" begins at nightfall and continues through the following day until sundown.

The Genesis account of creation repeats a rhythm our Creator set into motion. *"And there was evening and there was morning – the first day... the second day... Then God saw everything that He had made, and indeed it was very good. So, the evening and the morning were the sixth day."*[10] As I ponder this very different approach from our Western concept of the flow of the "day," sweet memories of evenings from when our boys were young flood my mind and heart.

As the sun dipped below the horizon, we'd gather around the oak table, give thanks for our meal, and enjoy a hearty dinner. The time was filled with jokes, laughter, and stories of the day. After clearing the dishes, we'd dive into games and, most nights, the boys would roll around and wrestle with their dad in the family room, while the house echoed with shrieks of laughter and playful growls. Next came bath time and comfy PJs. Snuggles on the couch with books and Bible stories filled the remainder of the evening. Last of all, with the boys tucked into bed, we'd pray together, thanking God for all the blessings in our lives, praying for protection over ourselves and our loved ones, and asking for peaceful sleep and good dreams. What a way to "start" the day!

I suspect our loving Father is much the same with us. He starts the day by providing for us — nourishing us with food, conversation, and joy. Then, as we rest, the Holy Spirit ministers to us through the night, strengthening and renewing us for the day ahead.

> *"It is vain for you to rise up early, to retire late,*
> *to eat the bread of painful labors;*
> *For He gives to His beloved even in his sleep."*
> ~ Psalm 127:2

While our bodies rest, our spirits are alive and alert and open for spirit-to-spirit communication. When we wake in the morning, the first twelve hours have already fortified us with food, fellowship, rest, and spiritual communion. With our identity securely established as the Father's beloved children in Christ Jesus, and from this place of abundance, we move forward into the second half of our day, doing the *"good works which God prepared beforehand that we should walk in them."* Ephesians 2:10.

> *"...He awakens me each morning;*
> *he awakens my ear to listen like those being instructed."*
> ~ Isaiah 50:4

Making the effort to understand God's metaphorical language in dreams opens a profound path to draw close to the heart of God. Time and again, Jesus tells his listeners *parables* inviting them into Kingdom truths and personal conviction. *"The one who has ears to hear, let them hear!"* He hasn't stopped speaking in parables, and His "night parables" in dreams draw us to seek Him for understanding. He is unimaginably generous, but He also calls us to actively seek Him.

A final thought on receiving God's communication to us. The more we break free from unhealthy patterns, destructive mindsets, and limiting relationships, the more receptive we become to the Father's guidance. For instance, in my life it wasn't just a left-brained, Greek-thinking culture that hampered my ability to process dreams metaphorically. It wasn't just a lack of practice. I was evaluating metaphorical messages through a lens of negativity and feeling less than. Perfectionism and comparison played a huge role in inhibiting my creative receptors. As my identity as a child of God becomes ever increasingly secure, my understanding of His language is ever expanding.

I believe there is much hope for accelerated maturing in the Body of Christ in the area of understanding and valuing dreams and the metaphorical communication of God. He is pouring out His Spirit on all flesh, and everywhere I look, I see a real hunger to hear from God and grow in understanding His ways.[11]

REFLECTIONS

1. How does the idea of God speaking through dreams challenge or affirm your understanding of His communication?

   _____

   _____

   _____

2. Have you dismissed a spiritual experience (yours or someone else's) because it didn't fit into your theological framework or comfort zone?

   _____

   _____

   _____

3. How does the shift from Greek to Hebrew thinking change your approach to reading and interpreting Scripture?

   _____

   _____

   _____

4. How has the rejection of certain spiritual gifts in the church affected your view of them? Have you ever felt pressured to reject something unfamiliar?

_____

_____

_____

5. Are there any unhealthy patterns, limiting relationships, or destructive mindsets that might be blocking you from receiving God's messages through dreams?

_____

_____

_____

Chapter 4

THE IMPORTANCE OF DREAMS TODAY

Our close friends, a family of six Jesus-loving, fiery reformers, had been fervently praying for God's direction regarding moving overseas as first-time missionaries. Many details needed to come together, significant financial provision was required, and the magnitude of this process was overwhelming. They had already faced numerous obstacles and setbacks along the way and found themselves at a major crossroads. They sensed they were supposed to go somewhere; there was constant nudging from the Lord, but they didn't know what or when. One night the dad had a dream.

> *"Our family was in a busy train station with people hustling each way to get to their own destination. We stood there not knowing what or where or even why we were supposed to be there. We put our old luggage down for them to load. We were told by someone that the next train was headed to Europe. When we looked at the train, we saw the destination, "Scotland," written on the engine. After we got on the train*

by faith, all of our luggage disappeared, and we were given new luggage. But not normal luggage. Super luxurious and expensive luggage covered in gold writing. And off we went."

> Dreams are one of the most effective ways God can communicate hidden or difficult truths to us.

The whole family was thrilled that their destination was indeed Scotland, a confirmation of the longing of their hearts. Through the dream, the Lord assured them that He would abundantly provide for them. In addition to the promises from the Word, the numerous confirming signs from the Lord, much prayer and counsel, and the support of their community, the dream provided them with an anchor, assuring them that their provision and destination were secure.

Why is it that a dream can have such a profound impact on our lives? What is it about dreams that can so powerfully encourage us in such a unique way? In its simplest form, a dream is a story, and God knows the power of a story. A parable. Dreams are one of the most effective ways God can communicate hidden or difficult truths to us. Especially truths we are consciously resistant to. King David is a great example of the power of a parable. He had committed adultery with his comrade's wife then had him killed to conceal his actions. You would think with a situation as egregious as this God would give a direct message to David through his spiritual adviser, Nathan the Prophet. Something like,

> *"Thus says the Lord - you have slept with the wife of one of your most trusted friends. You deserted him in battle, ensuring his death, all to cover your tracks. Repent!"*

Under God's direction, Nathan used a story, a parable, to open David's eyes to the gravity of his actions. David's newly awakened heart was cut to the quick. Like a defibrillator in a cardiac arrest, a parable jumpstarted him into repentance. He was consumed with remorse and realigned his heart to God.[12]

Dreams can be like that. They are, after all, "night parables." Stories that sneak up on us when we are asleep. Stories that God leverages to awaken us. In His incredible love He brings us back, empowers us to repent, and reminds us who we are.

Stories change lives, stories save lives. And who doesn't love a good story? Most of us have a favorite movie or a favorite book. How about a favorite TV series? I'm not sure if this is a good thing, but our family dinners often turn into a full-on quote fest from movies and shows we've watched.

How about some of culture's universally understood lines:

"Inconceivable!" "As you wish!" (The Princess Bride)
"May the force be with you" (Star Wars)
"You can't handle the truth!" (A Few Good Men)
"Houston, we have a problem" (Apollo 13)
"Show me the money!" (Jerry Maguire)
"It's just a flesh wound!" (Monty Python and the Holy Grail)

Take a minute to think about one of your favorites. Can you envision the scene? Hear the dialogue? Feel the emotion? Do you remember where you were, how you felt, how old you were when you first saw it? I distinctly remember standing for hours in a line that wound all the way around a Colorado Springs movie theater waiting to see the premier of Star Wars. The wonder of the groundbreaking pioneering work of George Lucas and the iconic sounds of John Williams have left an indelible impression.

Like a movie, one of the amazing things about dreams is their power to stick with us. They emotionally impact us, imprinting them on our souls. Dreams are often much more effective than reading a book or listening to a teaching, although both are necessary. In a dream, we are immersed in an experience that communicates a message.

As we mature in our understanding and value of dreams, the scope of their influence expands. When I first started evaluating dreams from a biblical perspective, I was only interested in *my* dreams and what they were revealing for *me* (and maybe my immediate family). Like a small child only focusing on what was in it for me. As the Lord continued to mature me, I started realizing that God was giving dreams to benefit others – individuals, families, communities, churches, cities, regions, and the world.

The scriptures are clear that God is always looking for someone to partner with Him to release on the earth what He intends from His Kingdom. Sure, He could do it on His own. But that's not what He's *chosen* to do. In Isaiah, He looked throughout the earth for someone, but there was no one.[13] So, He came Himself - as a human. Even through salvation, God partnered with someone on earth. Jesus!

"Kings and priests to our God" is what He has made those who are adopted through faith in Christ.[14] *We* are the ones with access to heaven's solutions for earth's problems! No one else on earth can do this! *We* are ministers of reconciliation.[15] Adam and Eve's original assignment has been restored to us – to have authority on earth establishing Kingdom principles that bring life and health to individuals, families, communities, systems, and countries.

Jesus was the first to use the word "Ekklesia" (church) in the context of the Kingdom of God, and Ekklesia is repeated 113 times in the New Testament.

*"Who do you say I am?" Simon Peter answered, "You are the Messiah, the Son of the living God." Jesus replied, "Blessed are you, Simon son of Jonah, for this was not revealed to you by flesh and blood, but by my Father in heaven. And I tell you that you are Peter, and on this rock, I will build my church (**Ekklesia**), and the gates of Hades will not overcome it. I will give you the keys of the kingdom of heaven; whatever you bind on earth will be bound in heaven, and whatever you loose on earth will be loosed in heaven."*

~ Matthew 16:18

Jesus released this declaration at a uniquely strategic location – literally, the "Gates of Hell." Recently, we toured Israel which included a trip to the Golan Heights in Caesarea Philippi. In the cliffs at the base of Mount Hermon stands a temple carved out of the stone, devoted to the gods Pan, Zeus, and Nemesis. It was believed that all gods came through a portal and entered earth in that location, wreaking havoc. We know these "gods" are in actuality evil principalities. It was the darkest of the dark places on the planet in Jesus' time. He wasn't referring to literal gates. In ancient times, a gate was a place where rulers met, and counsel was given. To control the gates of one's enemies was to conquer their city. He was referring to the demonically influenced culture, directed by these dark governing principalities. If we look around us today, we can see the very same forces at work.

The notion of Jesus creating His own Ekklesia was entirely new to His listeners. It might be a brand-new concept to much of the modern-day church as well. His disciples were looking for their Messiah to overthrow their oppressive government in the physical realm. God's ways had never occurred to them – that He didn't plan to do all the overcoming on His own. His ways were much more inclusive and powerful than they could have imagined.

You see, in that culture, the Greeks understood an Ekklesia to be an assembly of people authorized to *govern* the affairs of a city, state, or nation. To the Romans, an Ekklesia was a *governing body* sent into a conquered region, not only to govern, but to *alter the culture* until it became like Rome.

Jesus was describing the blueprints for a Body of people who would *exercise spiritual authority* and disciple nations for Him, extending His Kingdom rule on the earth. Their extension of Christ's Kingdom authority would be through the Holy Spirit empowerment of the gospel and by teaching and demonstrating the principles of His Kingdom in all spheres of society.

In other words, He designed *us* to govern with spiritual authority to alter the culture to look like His Kingdom. *We* are to invade darkness, *our* present-day gates of hell, with God's love, truth, solutions, light, and power, changing the culture to look like the Kingdom of heaven.

*"**You** are the salt of the earth...**You** are the light of the world."*
~ Matthew 5:13-14

We are in an era where targeted prayer strategy and direction are crucial as we advance against the gates of hell and set captives free. To do this, we need *real-time intel* from heaven. Dreams often release that intel for targeted prayer.

> We need *real-time intel* from heaven.

In the Word, the sons of Issachar were known for understanding the "signs of the times." The sons of Issachar were critical in strategy because they had intel on the current situation. They are forever honored as one of the tribes ushering in the line of David, the line of Christ, which became the line of eternity. Our lineage.

"And of the sons of Issachar, men who understood the times,
with knowledge of what Israel should do..."
~ 1 Chronicles 12:32

How about us? Are we asking to understand the signs of the times? God is the ultimate General and Master Planner for His creation. Many today are receiving God's perspective on current situations on the earth. Strategies to influence these current affairs with the Kingdom of Heaven. And much of that is occurring through dreams.

A dream shared with me a couple of years ago perfectly illustrates God releasing real-time intel and encouragement. Philipa Booyens, a talented screenwriter and passionate advocate for high-quality, clean, and empowering content in the arts and entertainment industry recently shared this dream with me.

Good old days 2.0

    I was in my parent's living room- a place I lived in from 13-18 years old. I was standing under my father's favorite chair facing the fireplace/hearth with a mantle and TV above it. The room was large, and I was small, like the size of a toy Barbie doll. I was standing under the cover of the chair with quite a somewhat small group of people I did not recognize but my grandfather was among them. He is a Korean War veteran and from the Silent GI Generation (born between 1926-1945). The room was quiet, nothing moved, but I got the feeling we were hiding from something, but I did not know what.

    The group I was with felt loosely organized and waiting. All of a sudden, we ran to the hearth and faced outwards towards the large red couch in my parents' living room. It had blankets on top of it and as I was staring at the couch, toy-sized soldiers started running over it towards us. They were armed and I knew they were enemies. My group took guard-like positions with weapons I had not realized we had and aimed at the toy-sized soldiers coming toward us. We took these soldiers down, but they kept coming over the couch towards us and many in our group started to go down as well. The stream of soldiers coming over the couch seemed to increase and seemed without end. There came a point where it was just my grandfather and me stationed defending my family's fireplace until my grandfather went down as well and there was just me remaining. I remember having to calmly focus and just keep shooting until the stream of incoming soldiers became a trickle that I just kept taking aim at and shooting until the incoming soldiers stopped.

    It was then that I realized we had won and all the people that were originally with me stood up (like they had come back to life), and they started celebrating with me. We went back under my father's favorite chair again as we continued to celebrate. Then

I was given a large cream-colored invitation. It was embossed with gold letters. It had TV show titles on it. One from the present, the next was a few decades earlier and the last was an old TV show. From present to earlier then even earlier. I turned the invitation over and it said in gold letters: good old days 2.0.

– *Philipa Booyens*

This dream played out like a full-color action film, vividly portraying the battle for hearth and home—and the influence of what enters through the television. Steady assault emerged from the stronghold of the couch, a place where families passively receive messaging through media. The oversized living room, contrasted with the toy-like figures battling within it, symbolized that this wasn't just about the dreamer's family, it represented the broader fight for families across the nation. The message rang loud and clear: even when outnumbered and all hope seemed lost, the dreamer persevered, and they emerged victorious. It wasn't just survival—it was a decisive triumph that ushered in *Good Old Days 2.0* What an amazing call to prayer, to boldly declare the message of victory from the dream, and to keep standing strong in the fight for families, arts, and entertainment.

When Jesus was tempted by the devil, He repelled the powerful seduction each time by speaking the Word of God.

"It is written: 'Man shall not live on bread alone,
but on every word that comes out of the mouth of God.'" [16]

I had always understood this to mean that we are to quote Scripture when tempted. And of course, with each temptation, Jesus replied with, "It is written." But when I studied this statement, to my surprise, the Greek for "word" in this statement is not *logos* but *rhema*. Although they have some overlapping meaning, they are not synonymous. In the Greek, the *logos* is a broader term that can mean speech, a message, reason, logic, or even Jesus Himself. It is different from *rhema*, which usually refers to a specific spoken word or saying.

I just love how Jesus said on repeat, *"You have heard it said, but I say..."* He is the living and breathing flesh and bone embodiment of Reality. He frequently turns our understanding of truth upside down and reveals a meaning we never even imagined. In that moment, Jesus poignantly brings the historical provision of manna into a fresh spiritual truth.

"He humbled you and let you be hungry and fed you with
manna which you did not know... that He might make you
understand that man does not live by bread alone, but man lives
by everything that proceeds out of the mouth of the Lord."
~ Deuteronomy 8:3

Notice how God humbled the Israelites by providing miraculous food that they couldn't produce for themselves. There's a lesson in this. Humility admits that we cannot feed ourselves. Hang in here with me as I explain. Yes, we can easily read and study the Word, listen to podcasts, stream our favorite teachers, and *think* we are receiving real sustenance. But we need fresh, daily, miraculous sustenance *from God Himself.* There's no storing rhema for later – the Israelites couldn't even save any for the next day.

The spiritual disciplines – prayer, reading / studying / hearing the Word of God, fasting, worship, serving, gratitude, and fellowship with other believers – all serve as the foundation to *position* us to receive *rhema* words from God. And always, the test of the authenticity of a "rhema" word is that it *must align* with the whole of Scripture.

So why all this talk of *rhema* words in a dream book? It just so happens that dreams are one of God's signature methods of communicating *rhema* words. Consider these history-making events that God *entrusted to a dream* to communicate a "now word" message. Many were for the immediate circumstances, while some foretold future events.

Through a dream, God:

- Spared a pagan king by revealing that the woman he planned to marry was already taken. (Genesis 20)
- Revealed God's mercy to this king by keeping him from consummating that marriage while she lived in his household (Genesis 20)
- Pointed out the reason for the king's wife and female servants' infertility, leading to their miraculous healing. (Genesis 20)
- Released a successful business strategy to Jacob (Genesis 31)
- Warned Jacob his time was up at his current work situation (Genesis 31)
- Protected Jacob by warning his father-in-law against payback when Jacob left without putting in his two-week notice. (Genesis 31)
- Foreshadowed a grand scale calling to Joseph (Genesis 37)
- Prepared an incarcerated wine steward for the reinstatement of his job (Genesis 40)
- Prepared an incarcerated baker for his impending death (Genesis 40)
- Preserved the bloodline of Christ by warning Pharoah of a famine on the heels of a period of unusual abundance. (Genesis 41)
- Divinely inspired interpretation ushered Joseph into his position as Prime Minister - fulfilling Joseph's calling dream (Genesis 41)
- Emboldened the family runt with an inferiority complex to obey God and take on an "unbeatable" army (Judges 7)
- Told a young king to ask for anything—he received mind-blowing wisdom and unimaginable wealth (I Kings 3)
- Predicted the progression of future kingdoms and ultimately the establishment of the Kingdom of God (Daniel 2)

- Warned a proud pagan king that if he didn't humble himself, he'd find himself living like a wild beast—no fairy tale ending in sight. (Daniel 4)
- Through revelation and correct interpretation, called off the executions of an entire division of "consultants" (Daniel 2)
- Reassured the earthly father of the Messiah that his fiancé genuinely was pregnant by the Holy Spirit (Matthew 1)
- Warned Joseph that Herod was after Jesus and told him to make a hasty exit for Egypt with his family and stay there until he got the all-clear. (Matthew 2)
- Saved Jesus' life, again, by giving Joseph the go-ahead to move back but diverting him to Nazareth for their safety (Matthew 2)
- Used his wife to warn a powerful governor to let Jesus go and gave him a chance to avoid being part of His death. (Matthew 27)

What a resume! What an incredible endorsement of God's confidence in releasing dreams to communicate critical information. What might happen if we actually took all of these biblical examples to heart and embraced dreams as one of God's "ways"? Exodus 33:13 is one of our "on repeat" prayers echoed as a request for a deeper and expanded understanding of the ways of God.

> *"Now therefore, if I have found favor in your sight,*
> *Please show me now your ways, that I may know you*
> *in order to find favor in your sight."*

While the Western church at large is ignoring dreams and dream interpretation, I can assure you that the world is not. They have plenty to say about these perplexing encounters. And, unfortunately, even believers are resorting to unclean sources to help them understand their dreams. Yet is it any wonder with so little teaching in the church? Where can they go to be discipled in God-centered, Bible-based dream interpretation?

The enemy is not a creator – his only move is to copy and distort God's ways. And he is happy to step in and offer his "insight" into the mysteries in dreams. But we know his tactics have one aim – to steal, kill and destroy.[17] Regrettably, many Christians are looking to Jungian, Freudian, or New Age dream interpretation methods for understanding. Jung himself even asserted that *he could never understand someone else's dream well enough to interpret it correctly*.[18] This contradicts both Joseph and Daniel who, while stating that only God knows the interpretation, proceeded to rely on God to help them accurately interpret the dreams of others.[19]

How can we be so confident these secular dream interpretation models are flawed? In addition to them being void of biblical principles, simply put, *they don't work*. If we apply their methods of dream interpretation to biblical dreams recorded, interpreted, and played out in history, we get the *wrong interpretation*.

Take Pharoah's dream featuring the seven fat cows and seven skinny cows, and the seven healthy grains and seven scorched grains. If Jungian or Freudian interpretation methods had been applied, they would have focused on the psychological state of the dreamer and completely missed the coming famine. The result? Jesus' bloodline would have been wiped out.

There is a great need for biblical dream interpretation training in the Body of Christ. And yet, I've encountered many who, while they intellectually agree to a doctrinal statement that embraces all the gifts of the Holy Spirit, are, in reality, strongly opposed to the *actual practice* of those gifts. Much is questioned. Attempts to make space for these gifts to operate are undermined in public gatherings.

Having the privilege of teaching dream interpretation in continuationist church communities,[20] I often hear statements such as, "There's no biblical example of studying and training to develop skill in dream interpretation." I've so appreciated my pastor's response in support of learning and growing in this skill: "Well, there's no example of studying to develop skill in preaching in scripture, but no one seems to have a problem with that."

The Importance of Training

Not long ago, I ran into a friend at a cafe, and she was having coffee with someone I'd never met before. She introduced me, telling her friend that she had attended my biblical dream interpretation seminars. In the course of our short conversation, her friend made an emphatic statement that she would *never* presume to help interpret someone else's dream - she would just tell them to pray about it and ask the Lord what it means. I could see that she was a mature and earnest believer. I got the sense that she was convinced her conviction came from a posture of humility and was in line with biblical principles.

I smiled and agreed that usurping someone's authority by insisting our interpretation is correct or that they follow our counsel doesn't align with Scripture. At the same time, I also assured her that 20 years ago, if someone had just told me to "pray about it," I would have walked away disheartened, not having a clue how to process my dream!

I went on to explain that helping one another with dreams is a biblical concept. That when Joseph encountered his discouraged fellow inmates, he first acknowledged that only God could interpret dreams. However, he then said, "Please, tell them to me."[21] He proceeded to help them correctly interpret their dreams. I went on to refer to Daniel, who asked his friends to pray with him to receive revelation about the king's dream. That night, the Lord revealed the mystery in a vision.[22]

I'm not sure if our conversation changed her perspective, but to me, it highlights the need for training in biblical dream interpretation. Can we receive revelation from God on the meaning of a dream without training? Yes, of course. However, studying and practicing interpretation develops *consistency*, which increases our ability to serve others more effectively.

When we recognize how highly the Lord values dreams as an essential means of communication, it's alarming how easily we've become comfortable dismissing this reality—and, in doing so, dismissing His ways. At its core, the issue of valuing what God values comes down to one thing: the fear of the Lord. Do we fear the Lord and reverence *all* His ways? Or do we consider our biblical world view like a smorgasbord, picking and choosing what suits our taste? Or what is familiar to us?

> Studying and practicing interpretation develops *consistency*, which increases our ability to serve others more effectively.

I encourage each of us to ask the Lord to show us areas where we might be "picky eaters," not valuing what He values. As we read the word, meditate, and pray, let's ask the Holy Spirit to highlight His ways. To help us see where we are aligned with His purposes and where we are neglecting them. And because He will surely reveal Himself to us, let's commit to deepening our understanding in the areas where we're lacking.

REFLECTIONS

1. Why do you think many in the Church accept training for gifts like preaching but resist training for others, like dream interpretation? How can that mindset be shifted?

_____

_____

_____

2. How does Jesus' use of the term *Ekklesia* change your understanding of what "church" is meant to be? What is your current understanding of our authority to alter culture to look like the Kingdom of Heaven?

_____

_____

_____

3. Why is it crucial to trust God's scriptural principles in dream interpretation over secular methods?

_____

_____

_____

4. Do you believe that God can give you "rhema" words in dreams, just as He did for people throughout Scripture?

_____

_____

_____

5. How do you currently view the connection between dreams and God's will for your life? What might need to shift in your mindset to see dreams as an essential part of your journey with the Lord?

_____

_____

_____

Chapter 5

SOURCES OF DREAMS

Every dream is an invitation to connect with God.

"All revelation and it's interpretation belongs to God."
~ Genesis 40:8

Dream:

> *I was driving along a road near our neighborhood. In my rearview mirror, I saw a police vehicle with flashing lights. I was being pulled over. At the nearest side street, I turned off the main road, stopped, and prepared to talk with the officer who had pulled in behind me. Suddenly, the officer raced off to answer another call. I was relieved he didn't give me a ticket.* End of dream.

Believing this to be a warning dream, when I awoke, I made a mental note to be careful behind the wheel. That mental note must have been written on some defective 3M adhesive because it didn't last long. Midmorning, I pulled out of our driveway onto our deserted neighborhood street. I drove slowly, meandering as I applied my mascara and put lipstick on. (I know, I know. I shouldn't put makeup on while driving.) After a couple of turns, I noticed flashing lights behind me. I slowed to a stop on the side of the residential street. I had no idea why he was stopping me - I knew I wasn't speeding.

Then I remembered the dream and thought, "In the dream, I didn't get a ticket," so I relaxed. The officer approached and asked for my license and registration and informed me I hadn't signaled any of my turns. He then added, "Ma'am, I've had my lights on while you made two turns. Did you not see me?" My face grew red as I admitted that I was distracted. (I had made sure the mascara and lipstick were stowed away in my purse.) He checked my information on his computer, returned, and let me off with a warning to be more mindful while I was driving. Just like the dream.

Similarly, *I dreamt that my husband, Dave, was unreasonably detained by a sheriff and the officer was harassing him for inconsequential things. The lighting was bright and colors vivid. In the dream, I stood next to him while this exchange was going on, frustrated at the abuse of power. Eventually the officer relented and went on his way.*

Dave left early that morning for a meeting, and I awoke while he was en route. I put on the coffee and was switching a load of laundry when I suddenly remembered the dream. I quickly called to warn him. He answered with an abrupt, "I can't talk right now. I just got pulled over." I prayed for him while I waited for a return call, but noted that in the dream, he didn't get a ticket. Twenty minutes later, he called back and related the story of being pulled over for speeding but not being given a ticket, just like the dream.

Although these "heads up" dreams were not life-altering revelations, I believe they are more than just humorous anecdotes. These dreams serve to illustrate that God really does care about the day-to-day minutia of our lives.

God, however, isn't the only source of our dreams. I have found it curious that simply mentioning dream interpretation in a conversation with a conservative believer often evokes this question: "Do you think all dreams are from God?" The answer, which is "no, not all dreams are from God," would be basic understanding in the Eastern culture. (Incidentally, I've never heard an unbeliever ask this question.) My experience is that it seems to be a big question among Christians in the Western church. Why is that?

This common concern reveals a profound gap in understanding in the Western church. I was no exception the first 30 years of my life. As discussed in Chapter 3, for various reasons, we lack awareness of or even a general framework for dreams, much less their importance within the boundaries of scriptural principles. A genuine suspicion of participating in something New Age is totally justified. But if we are truly wanting God to show us His ways, we have to become reconciled to His biblical communication patterns and how He doesn't change.[23]

If you're feeling fear about practicing dream interpretation, even through a biblical lens, I encourage you to pray and step out in faith. Any approach that is motivated by fear is not from God. Fear of "getting it wrong" or "making mistakes" just reveals a need for the steadying, assuring, unconditional love of God in our lives. This is His invitation:

"There is no fear in love. But perfect love drives out fear, because fear has to do with punishment. The one who fears is not made perfect in love."
~ 1 John 4:18

I've talked with many believers who, in theory, agree that all operations of the Holy Spirit are for today, yet respond to the actual training in and practicing of these gifts with statements like, "I'm open, but cautious." While this might appear to be wisdom, it completely lacks scriptural backing. My response has been, "Don't be cautious, be discerning." We are, after all, talking about *gifts from God*. And we know that every gift that God gives is good.[24]

As we follow Jesus with our whole heart, soul, mind, and strength, we're encouraged to,

"Pursue love, and earnestly desire the spiritual gifts."
~ 1 Corinthians 14:1

Circling back to answer our original question, "No, not all dreams are from God." However, every kind of dream, even if it isn't from God, *is* an invitation to connect with Him. Our dreams come from one of four sources. Three are spiritual sources and one is physical:

Dreams from **God**
Dreams from our **Soul**
Dreams from the **Enemy**
Dreams affected by our **Body**

Dreams from **God**

*"... I, the Lord, **reveal myself to them in visions, I speak to them in dreams.**"*
~ Numbers 12:6

*"In the last days, God says, I will pour out my Spirit on **all people**. Your sons and daughters will prophesy, your young men will see visions, **your old men will dream dreams.** Even on my servants both men and women, I will pour out my Spirit in those days, and they will prophesy."*
~ Acts 2:17

When God is the source, our dreams are typically filled with light and color. Not a hard and fast rule, but a helpful indicator. Only one source of light exists, and that is our Eternal Creator. When Yahweh made a covenant with Noah, He sealed it by displaying a rainbow in the sky, white light refracted to reveal the entire color spectrum. John put it this way,

"This is the message we have heard from him and declare to you:
God is light; in him there is no darkness at all."
~ 1 John 1:5

John personally saw the Throne of God and described it as exploding with light and color.

"...and around the throne was a rainbow that
had the appearance of an emerald."
~ Revelation 4:3, 5

Another characteristic of God as the source is that only dreams from God accurately tell us of future events. This is because only God knows the future. Time exists within God; He is the Alpha and Omega, and only He sees the end from the beginning. Pharaoh's dream about seven abundant years followed by seven years of famine, for example, could not have originated from himself or the enemy because neither can tell the future. (Think about it. The enemy does not know the future. If he did, he would never have crucified Jesus when the Lord laid His life down. Look how that turned out for him!)

> A dream from God will ALWAYS line up with His character, but not always with OUR current understanding of Him.

A dream from God will ALWAYS line up with His character, but not always with OUR current understanding of Him. Even with a casual glance at the dreams recorded in the Bible, it becomes apparent that not all dreams from God leave us feeling all warm and fuzzy. Yes, it's true that many dreams from God encourage us, release a strategy for our circumstances, give a promise of His destiny for us, or remind us of His steadfast love.

Sometimes, however, these dreams are warnings, correction, or a call to action. In Job 33, the writer describes how God opens our ears *"and with a warning, terrifies them..."* in order to keep us from pride and even from death.[25] In it, He might reveal a scheme of the enemy. He might show us an area in which we need to repent. He might direct us away from a destructive path.

A great biblical example of this is the dream the Lord gave Pilate's wife while Jesus was on trial.

> *"While court was still in session, Pilate's wife sent him a message:*
> *'Don't get mixed up in judging this noble man. I've just been through*
> *a long and troubled night because of a dream about him.'"*
> ~ Matthew 27:19

Imagine how different Pilate's life might have been if he had paid attention to the wisdom in that dream. (I like to joke, "or if he'd just listened to his wife.") He could have spared himself the torment of having a hand in crucifying Jesus. But the fear of man led him to resist allowing the communication from heaven to alter his course.

> When God is the source, our dreams are typically filled with light and color.

I once had a dream I knew was a warning not to discuss a topic with an individual or it would result in them reacting in defensive anger. Want to hear *how* I know this was the correct interpretation? I didn't heed the warning, brought it up anyway, and the disastrous result played out just like the dream. Lesson learned. Hopefully.

Although not pleasant, warning dreams are absolutely the Father's love in action toward us. They are an invitation into obedience, leading to the flourishing life Jesus promised us. In fact, these corrective dreams are truly a great reason to give thanks. We can circumvent pitfalls that are hidden from us. We can avoid engaging with unsafe people, just like the Wise men who were warned not to return to Herod.[26] God can reveal sin and the dire consequences, like He did for Nebuchadnezzar,[27] giving us an opportunity to repent. Hidden areas of pride in our lives we often label as "justified" can be revealed and renounced. Our God is a jealous Bridegroom and is relentless in rooting out whatever causes distance and keeps us from the fullness of our destiny.

"God opposes the proud but gives grace to the humble."
~ James 4:6

I don't know about you, but I'd like to avoid delays caused by pride in my life.

When the source of a dream is God, regardless of the type of dream, one consistent characteristic is that they always leave us with *hope*. God dreams, even correction dreams, come with solutions, not no-win scenarios. He always provides a path forward.

Dreams from our **Soul** (Mind, Will, and Emotions)

The **soul** also has the ability to generate dreams. Dreams generated from our souls are typically muted in color, not filled with the pure light of God. Jeremiah warns us not to give weight to these types of dreams.

"For thus says the LORD of hosts, the God of Israel:
Do not let your prophets and your diviners who are in your midst deceive you,
*nor listen to **your dreams which you cause to be dreamed."***
~ Jeremiah 29:8

They are generated from our mind, our will, and our emotions, apart from the influence of the Spirit of God. A "soul" dream originates from our own will, carnal desires, deception, ungodly mindsets, anxieties, etc. In other words, they are self-generated.

That being said, it's important to understand that our souls are not inherently bad. With our souls we feel emotion, we choose what to do or believe, we house our memories. Within our souls resides what makes us unique - our personalities, quirks, passions, memories, and intellect. We experience the heart of the Father in our souls.

Mary praised God with her soul *and* with her spirit,

"My soul magnifies the Lord, and my spirit rejoices in God my Savior…"
~ Luke 1:46, 47

The soul responds to the leading of our spirit. If we renew our minds, feed on the word of God and the Presence of His spirit, our soul functions in beautiful service under the authority of the Holy Spirit. An unyielded soul, indulged and overly fed, can manifest as we sleep. Anxiety ridden scenarios and lust driven scenes fill our dreams.

> God dreams, even correction dreams, come with solutions, not no-win scenarios.

When it comes to the ruling influence in our lives, the biblical model is our soul submitted to the rule of our spirit. Our spirits perceive the Holy Spirit's revelation and guidance, and our spirit then informs our soul and body.

"If we walk by the spirit, we will not carry out the deeds of the flesh."
~ Galatians 5:16

There is an upside to a soul dream, however. It can reveal issues that have not yet been surrendered to the Lordship of Jesus Christ, which is super helpful. Once again, this kind of dream is an invitation to draw closer to the Lord in repentance and surrender. A soul dream is a call to renew trust, re-anchor in our identity as sons and daughters, and to saturate ourselves in the Father's perfect love. A soul dream can motivate us to strengthen our spirit.

Dreams from the **Body**

Our dreams can be influenced by our bodies as well. A high fever, a virus, pregnancy, physical exhaustion, or pharmaceuticals can affect our sleep and our dreams. Once after enduring a night of nightmarish scenes and semi-conscious anxiety as the result of taking Nyquil, I texted my sister, my fellow vivid dreamer.

"Does Nyquil affect your dreams?" I asked.

Without hesitation she responded, *"Nyquil is from the devil!"*

We had a good laugh over that. And while most people don't have a reaction to the medications in Nyquil, I can assure you that I haven't touched it since.

Dreams from the **Enemy**

Speaking of the devil, there are certain dreams that are clearly influenced by evil forces. These simply cannot have originated from God, our souls, or our bodies. Nightmares, dreams with terrifying no-win scenarios, for example, are not from God. James describes God's gift-giving character, *"Every good and perfect gift is from above, coming down from the Father of the heavenly lights, who does not change like shifting shadows."*[28]

> A soul dream is a call to renew trust, re-anchor in our identity as sons and daughters, and to saturate ourselves in the Father's perfect love.

If certain dreams don't come from God, or our souls, or our bodies, logically there must be a fourth source of dreams - the adversary. Jesus told us, *"the enemy comes to steal, kill, and destroy."*[29] The way the demonic realm does this in dreams is by harassing through promoting fear, terror, and deception.

These disturbing dreams engender a feeling of helplessness and anxiety. False dreams often entice us to believe something from the enemy is really from the Lord. Zechariah warned that demons, evil forces, are a source of false dreams.

> *"For the idols speak delusion; the diviners envision*
> *lies and tell false dreams…".*[30]

We know from 2 Timothy that God has *not* given us a spirit of fear, and therefore a dream designed to horrify us and leave us with no hope would not be from Him.[31] It would also make no sense for our souls to engender that type of terror.

When we face a nightmare, it's an invitation to turn to the Father for comfort. We also can take authority over the dark realm in the name and by the blood of Jesus.

> *"…and gave them power and authority over all*
> *the demons and to heal diseases."*
> ~ Luke 9:1

If you do have a nightmare, one of the best ways to turn it back on the enemy's head is to "flip the dream." Take the message of the nightmare and declare the opposite. For instance, if you have a dream where you are being chased down a dark alley and there is no way out. Flip the dream by declaring the opposite. James 4:6–8 says,

> *"God opposes the proud, but gives grace to the humble.*
> *Therefore, submit to God. But resist the devil and he will flee*
> *from you. Come near to God and he will come near to you."*

If you encounter a nightmare, turn it back on the enemy and "flip the dream" declaring the opposite.

So, stand firmly on the truth of Scripture—declare that the enemy is a defeated foe, that you are holding your ground against his intimidation, and that God is near. Also, with this kind of fear inducing dream, ask God to help you turn and face the intimidator telling it to go in Jesus' name. Call on the Lord for justice in your life after enduring the terror of the nightmare.

There is, however, an exception to the source of frightening dreams. As we learned previously, Job 33 reveals that God, in a Father's kindness, will terrify us in a dream for our own good.

"In a dream in a vision of the night, when deep sleep falls on people as they slumber in their beds, He may speak in their ears and terrify them with warnings, to turn them from wrongdoing and keep them from pride, to preserve them from the pit, their lives from perishing by the sword. God does all these things to a person—twice, even three times - to turn them back from the pit, that the light of life may shine on them."
~ Job 33:14-18, 29-30

Notice that there is *hope* with this type of dream from God. Very different from a dream from the enemy. The Lord's goal is abundant life for us to:

- turn us from destructive behavior
- keep us from pride (remember God resists the proud, which causes delays.[32])
- keep us from physical death
- save our souls
- bring us back to life-giving ways, to walk in God's light

A final note on sources of dreams. It is not uncommon to have a dream from God transition into something more sinister. I've experienced this as have others I've encountered. Just as in life, a well-known tactic of the enemy is to steal God's message through distraction or intimidation—and the same strategy can show up in our dreams. Hang onto the dream from God and ignore the interference of the enemy.

> Call on the Lord for justice in your life after enduring the terror of the nightmare.

Every kind of dream is an invitation to process with Holy Spirit no matter the source of a dream. Soul dreams that arise from our own anxieties (being chased or falling, for example), invite us to go to the Comforter to *"pray, request, and give thanks"* Philippians 4:6,7.[33] Even nightmares are an opportunity to flex our spiritual muscles by taking authority.[34] A nightmare causes us to run to our Strong Tower for help and protection.[35] The nature of a nightmare can provide valuable insight into the tactics and schemes of the enemy.

Regardless of the type of dream you experience, determine to make the most of it. A great question to ask upon waking is, "God what can you show me about Yourself, about me, and about the world around me through this dream?"

REFLECTIONS

1. What are some practical ways you can discern whether a dream is from God, our soul, the enemy, or our body?

_____

_____

_____

2. What role does fear play in your response to dreams, and how can you overcome it in order to grow in discernment and faith?

_____

_____

_____

3. In what ways can God use a seemingly negative or unsettling dream (such as a warning or correction) to draw you closer to Him and shape our character?

_____

_____

_____

4. How can you distinguish between a warning dream and one that might be a product of anxiety or a physical condition?

_____

_____

_____

5. How would you describe the difference between being "cautious" and being "discerning"?

_____

_____

_____

Chapter 6

CATEGORIES OF DREAMS

"When we know the category of the drama we've experienced, anxiety dissipates, clarity emerges, and hope is free to shine."

In 2012, I had a vivid dream that gave me a chilling taste of terror—an experience so intense, it carved itself into my memory forever.

I was running for my life. There were many of us frantically trying to run to any place we could find to hide. Although it was dark, it was impossible to conceal ourselves. Each of us was on our own - we had no companion for comfort or help. We were each wearing baby blue, and we had been marked for death. I tried running to the hills, but "they" found me. I climbed in a hope chest, but "they" knew where I was hiding. I had no voice and no one to protect me. Eventually, out of options, I stood helplessly in the foyer of an old Victorian type house in front of a man who was assigned to kill me. I was utterly powerless. I knew I would die in one of several ways. He could poison me, and that would be a slow, excruciating death. He could shoot me, but I might survive and be permanently maimed. Another form of execution involved searing pain. I was absolutely frozen with terror as the scene faded into darkness.

Next, I found myself floating near the ceiling of the parlor of that same house. The room was dingy with muted colors and full of people mingling and socializing. I was invisible to everyone in the room except for one person. Sitting listlessly in the corner, a young woman could see me - feel my presence. I knew I had died and that we were separated with no way to communicate. I was completely alone.

In the last scene I found myself even more terrified than in the first two. The theme had shifted. Somehow, I was alive again and I was walking along a quiet suburban neighborhood street at night. In the glow of streetlamps, I saw a hideous, huge demon-like creature stalking in my direction. Slung over its shoulder was a lifeless, freshly slaughtered red horse. The murderous alien-like creature was so enormous that the horse looked to be the size of a bloody hound dog on its shoulder. Panic surged through me as it advanced with heavy, giant-like strides— quickly devouring the distance between us. Bracing for an attack, I tensed—only to feel a rush of relief as it thundered past, its massive frame bumping my shoulder and scraping hard against my arm."

I bolted awake, heart pounding and shaking from fear. For the next few days, I was literally afraid to go to sleep, something I hadn't felt since God healed me of nightmares. I was bewildered. Why would I have such a nightmare? I went to the Lord for comfort and asked Him to cleanse me. I prayed for understanding. I shared the dream with Dave and a few close friends. As elements of the dream began to piece together, I came to the sickening realization that I had encountered a fraction of what the unborn child experiences in the moments before it is aborted. I witnessed the mother in the aftermath, empty and alone in her awareness of the loss of her child. The monster perpetuating all this death was on display, roaming through suburbia stripping away the God-given authority every woman is born to possess.

The timing of the dream proved to be strategic. Later that week, we hosted members of the Justice House of Prayer led by Matt Lockett. They were in town for a Lou Engle prayer gathering with the ending of abortion in America as their focus.

As I talked with Matt about this dream, he asked me to describe the "monster," and I showed him an illustration an artist friend had drawn from my description. To my astonishment, he informed me that this was the same manifestation God had shown others in their dreams about the evil power behind abortion.

> Knowing what type of dream we've experienced is key to understanding its meaning.

Turns out this dream wasn't a nightmare from the enemy, after all. God gave me this dream, a "calling dream" propelling me into focused intercession to end abortion in our country. Within two years I began co-writing a book on the life of Dr. Bernard Nathanson, the "Abortion king," and how the lies and devaluing of life had profoundly affected him, my co-author Lisa Kratz Thomas, myself, and the nation.[36]

Dream Categories

Knowing what type of dream we've experienced is key to understanding its meaning. As always, we rely on the Holy Spirit to reveal the meaning. However, it's not uncommon to mis-categorize a dream and bias the interpretation. A soul dream, engendered from our strong desires, can be seen as a directional message from the Lord. A clear example of this would be dreaming that a particular individual is our future spouse. (It's possible this type of dream could be from the Lord but often is from our intense longings.) In the same way, a skewed view of the Father and our worth in His eyes can morph what is meant as an encouraging dream from Him into believing it is a correction dream.

The Bible includes various categories of dreams, each with its own purpose and significance. It's worth noting that some of these are visions—similar to dreams—in which the message is communicated through vivid visual imagery. Let's take a closer look at these different types. The following list is borrowed heavily from Michael Wise and John Paul Jackson's "Top 20 Categories of Dreams."[37] I highly recommend this unique resource.

Dreams to Fulfill God's Call on Your Life

Prophecy and Revelation Dreams – Joseph's dream of the sheaves of wheat, sun, moon, and stars bowing down to him (Genesis 37:5-11). Pharaoh's dreams foretold the coming years of abundance followed by famine (Genesis 41:1-7).

Calling Dreams – Through Jacob's ladder dream, God confirms that Abraham's promises will be fulfilled through Jacob's descendants (Genesis 28:11-18).

Courage Dreams –Gideon overheard a dream in the enemy camp that assured him they would win the battle (Judges 6:9-15).

Direction Dreams – Joseph's dream confirms the truth of Mary's account, encouraging him to believe in her and move forward with their marriage (Matthew 1:18-25). The Magi were directed through a dream not to revisit Herod and return home by another route (Matthew 2:12).

Inventions Dreams – Jacob received a business strategy for increasing his herds (Genesis 31:9-13). Einstein's Theory of Relativity was released in a dream.

Words of Knowledge Dreams – Joseph received a word of knowledge that King Herod was dead (Matthew 2:13).

Dreams for Course Correction

Correction Dreams – When Peter saw a sheet let down with unclean animals and told to eat, his theology was corrected in a single day (Acts 10).

Warning Dreams – Joseph was warned by an angel in a dream to get up and flee to Egypt with Mary and Jesus (Matthew 2:13, 14).

Current-Condition Dreams – Nebuchadnezzar's dream of the great tree being cut down and bound for 7 years. Daniel urges him to change his ways – to humble himself and be kind to the oppressed (Daniel 4). This was also a correction dream and a warning dream. A current condition dream shows us how we view ourselves, and how we view God, or gives a clarifying picture of our circumstances.

Dreams for Healing and Transformation

Healing Dreams – These dreams invite us into relational, physical, emotional, and spiritual healing. (Joseph's relationship with Mary was healed through a dream, Matthew 1:20,21.)

Deliverance Dreams – Peter and the sheet let down delivered him from a religious spirit (Acts 10).

Flushing Dreams – Dreams that "flush" defilement from interactions, environments, or things let in through the eye-gate.

Dreams from the Enemy

Dark Dreams – Job's friend spoke of dark dreams. In his dream, a spirit glided past his face and made his bones shake and his hair stand on end. The message from this spirit was not from God (Job 4:12-19).

False Dreams – In Zechariah 10:2, Zechariah reveals that "idols" (or the demonic realm) speak delusion and engender false dreams.

Fear Dreams – Nightmares are from the enemy and are sent to terrorize, steal sleep, and make an individual fearful of dreams. These are no win situations leaving the dreamer distressed and without hope. In children, they are an attempt to shut down their abilities in the unseen realm.

Body and Chemical Dreams

Chemical Dreams – Dreams that arise from the interaction between chemical influences and the brain.

Body Dreams – Our physical state can influence our dreams. Pregnancy can affect a mother's dreams, both influenced by hormonal changes and by her baby's dreams. Pain from an injury or fever from an illness can result in distressing dreams. Ecclesiastes 5:3[38] describes vexation in dreams as a result of physical overwork and mental obsession. Contrast this to Ecclesiastes 5:12[39] which says that the sleep from a hard day's work is sweet.

No matter the category of dream, the very ability to dream is a gift from God. By design, we're all created with the fascinating reality of dreaming, and stepping into the journey of stewarding this universal experience is truly an adventure. Each dream is an opportunity to engage with the Lord, seeking His wisdom and perspective. What a beautiful invitation into connection with our King.

REFLECTIONS

1. Why is it important to correctly identify the category of a dream before interpreting it, and how can mis-categorizing a dream lead to misunderstanding its message?

_____

_____

_____

2. How does the variety of dream categories in Scripture demonstrate God's desire to engage with you through multiple aspects of your life?

_____

_____

_____

3. How can your personal desires or biases influence how you interpret dreams, and what are some ways to guard against misinterpreting dreams based on these emotions?

_____

_____

_____

4. What role does your relationship with God play in categorizing the types of dreams you experience?

_____

_____

_____

5. How can understanding different dream categories impact the way you approach and pray about our dreams, especially when they involve significant life decisions?

_____

_____

_____

Chapter 7

PRACTICAL TOOLS FOR RECORDING A DREAM

"Dreams are night parables written in disappearing ink."
~ John Paul Jackson

Dream:

In my dream, I was somewhere with food. End of dream.

My friend Lori, who introduced me to the value of dreams, emailed me this short dream. When I read it, I burst out laughing, and we ended up sharing a good laugh about it over the phone. No major plot or details. Just "somewhere with food." Incidentally, this same friend once sent me a birthday card with a guy flying through the sky on a roll of toilet paper - her added text read, "If this was your dream, what does this vehicle mean?" But I digress.

Of course, it seems silly to write down just that snippet of a dream, doesn't it? Why even bother, right? Well, it so happened that she entered an unanticipated season of travel with an undetermined itinerary, and the Lord provided physically, emotionally, and spiritually all along the way. So, it turns out she *was* "somewhere" with "food." I put that lesson in my pocket – no matter how insignificant a dream feels or how little I remember, be faithful to record it.

"The one who is faithful in a very little thing is also faithful in much..."
~ Luke 16:10

A few years back, I served as an intercessor for some leaders in full-time ministry. Consequently, as a dreamer, I had multiple dreams involving some of these leaders and their families. I received quite a few dreams for one particular family. Over the years, I would share these dreams with them for encouragement or potential insight. One day, they reached out and asked if I'd be willing to compile and send them the dreams the Lord had given me for them.

I readily agreed but immediately broke out in a sweat as a wave of anxiety washed over me. Don't get me wrong. It wasn't that I was reluctant to send the dreams. I was happy to. *Finding* all the dreams - that was the real challenge.

I spent the better part of an afternoon and evening searching through multiple journals, my three-ring "dreams" binder, and I'll admit, some loose random papers I'd scribbled various dreams on. Ok, organization may not be my strongest quality. Eventually I gathered them all, digitized the dreams in a document and sent them along.

That's the day I decided to record all of my dreams digitally. Lesson learned.

Speaking of recording dreams, have you ever had a vivid dream and just *know* you'll remember it, only to have the details slip away before finishing your morning coffee? I've never met anyone who hasn't had that experience. John Paul Jackson coined this brilliant phrase,

"Dreams are night parables written in disappearing ink."

Let me just say, I get it—deciding to take the time and effort to record your dreams can feel daunting! But let me encourage you: it's worth it. When you commit to remembering and recording your dreams while conversing with God about them, it unlocks a whole new dimension of intimacy with the Creator. And, if we are valuing what God values, stewarding dreams becomes a natural priority. It's worth repeating.

"God is literally leaving diamonds under our pillows at night,
and we are throwing them away."
~ Matt Lockett of Justice House of Prayer DC

The first step in stewarding a dream is determining to record it somehow. So, make your best effort to record any dream as soon as you can upon waking. The tricky thing about recording dreams, however, is that they take place unbound by space, time, and the laws of gravity. When you dive into recording them, you quickly discover that you are *translating*.

Over the years, I have kept track of dreams in a variety of different ways which I'll detail below. Taking advantage of different methods of recording will help you grasp the "shape and feel" of the dream.

These days, my preferred method is to voice to text into a "notes app" on my phone. Later, I go back and edit them and then transfer them to a Word document. I used to write them out by hand, and because the physical act of writing engages the right brain, it is a preferred method. Many of my friends simply voice record their dreams and later transfer them to paper or a document. My husband, an engineer, writes out his dreams with a pen on engineering paper. Always.

If you do take pen to paper, my hat is off to you!

Document Your Dream

Here are a few suggested ways to document a dream:

- Write out the dream in story form (probably the most common).
- Voice-record the dream. (The downside of this method is the difficulty in finding specific details within a long recording.)
- Ignore complete sentences and free-flow the events of the dream.
- Cluster diagram the main elements (see diagram below).
- Bullet point the main aspects of the dream.
- Write out the "feel" of the dream.
- Write the dream in a spiral, starting in the center of the paper and circling outward. This taps into the creative power of the right brain.
- Draw in an illustration the major elements and sequence of the dream. Cheers to all of you artists and cartoonists out there. The best I've done is stick figures.

Once you have the dream recorded in some form, document these elements as well:

- Title the dream
- Date the dream
- Determine who or what is the *focus* of the dream
- Note who/what the *sub-focuses* are
- Note the *details* – location, time period, weather elements, animals, numbers, colors, etc.
- Assign a category to the dream
- Write the interpretation you believe God is giving you

Easy-peasy, right? Well, maybe not exactly. If you're anything like me, it's not as simple as it sounds. A dream often contains a number of strange elements with a healthy dose of emotion thrown in. Often, many of the elements are difficult to describe. Distinguishing between the main focus, sub-focuses, and details can be a challenge. I remember thinking, "But everything seems like the focus!"

Hang in there. It does get easier with practice. Let's take a look at determining the focus, sub-focuses, and details of a dream.

Focus

Who or what is the **focus** of the dream? Often, the dreamer will conclude that the focus of the dream is someone else and home in on that aspect. But many dreams we think are *about others* are in fact *about us*, or at least partially a communication for us.

When determining the focus of a dream, a helpful question to ask is, "What is my part in this dream?" Here's a tip: Try removing yourself from the dream entirely—does the storyline fall apart? If it does, you're likely the focus or at least a key part of it.

Are you active in the dream or just watching? If you are primarily observing, the dream is most likely giving revelation about others or a given situation. But if you are active in the majority of a dream, no matter how others are involved, the dream is giving revelation, in some respect, about you, especially in that given context.

Another possibility is that you may represent someone or something else in the dream as a major focus. For instance, I often represented intercession and practicing the gifts of the Spirit when I would have a dream featuring a ministry I was personally connected to.

Many have been experiencing dreams related to our nation and the Church in this season. These dreams have detailed assistance from the angelic realm, areas of darkness, hidden realities, and prayer strategies. In these dreams, various leaders may represent a particular movement or aspect of the Body of Christ, or the country. For instance, a national prayer leader would likely represent the prayer movement. A well-known pastor could represent pastors in general.

That being said, if the focus is not the dreamer, the focus will be the major "player" or "players" of the dream. For example:

> *My husband and I are approaching our daughter and son-in-law's house. They're seated in the living room with their young kids and the walls are clear so I can see inside the house. As we approach it, we see a large alligator stick his head through the side door and snarl at us. It then makes its way through the house to where everyone is sitting. A man takes our oldest granddaughter's hand and gives her a pickax. She easily lifts it and smashes it on the head of the alligator and kills it. She is calm and matter of fact and the man disappears. Our daughter and her husband are really pleased to see her handle it so efficiently. They didn't even move from their positions seated on the couch.* - B.H.

Although the dreamer is the grandparent, the dream is about her daughter's family, and in particular her oldest granddaughter. "My interpretation is that my daughter and son-in-law lead transparent lives (see-through walls and windows), but even still the enemy is still always prowling around and looking for a way to get close enough to harm them. My granddaughter knows how to receive from the Lord and knows what to do with that information (in this case crush the enemy). Her parents remain at rest and trust that the Lord will provide what their children need to combat the enemy."

Like this dream, something I've consistently noticed in my dreams is that when I'm in someone else's house, it's often the Lord highlighting something about them. These dreams usually serve as a prompt for encouragement or intercession, leading me to pray for them.

Sub-Focus

Determining the **sub-focuses** of a dream helps to provide context and key information. To do this, it's helpful to ask, "who or what are the *other* main characters?" If the other main elements are people, ask yourself:

What do they represent to me?

What does their name mean?

Are they a reoccurring person in my dream?

Remember, dreams are metaphorical. They are parables. It's tempting to interpret the message of a dream based on the literal person featured in it. Yet, the meaning of a name, not the person, could very well serve as a key to unlocking the interpretation of a dream. Recurring characters are definitely an invitation to partner with the Lord, unraveling that mystery together. It's like He's leaving clues to a treasure. It's a great opportunity to dig deeper into recurring characters and discover the significance behind them. I've had multiple dreams where Pierce Brosnan played a key role. When I'd wake up and tell Dave that Pierce Brosnan was in my dream, he'd raise an eyebrow, silently asking, "Seriously, again?" It became a bit of a running joke. In these dreams, Pierce usually played the role of the hero—showing up to save the day. In one, he was throwing a football with my boys on the beach. In another, he and my husband were building a staircase in our home. Over time, it became clear what Pierce was representing - none other than *Jesus*!

One evening, while teaching a dream seminar, I was sharing this reoccurring figure as an illustration when a participant offered additional insight. He pointed to the center of each of his palms and

> The meaning of a name, not the person, could very well serve as a key to unlocking the interpretation of a dream.

said, "Pierced." As in, Jesus was *pierced* for our transgressions. Tears filled my eyes with a fresh revelation. I was overwhelmed by the Father's love in crafting these dreams just for me.

Although a sub-focus may be embodied by a person, sub-focuses can also be a place or structure, like a city or a building. For instance, if the dream takes place in your grandma's house, the theme may involve generational aspects of your life. The setting may be a church or the workplace. Another country or even outer space can be the backdrop, offering context as a sub-focus. If the dream is played out in a previous era, it may be pointing to something that took place in that time of history that is influencing the present. All of these settings serve as sub-focuses and help to offer information and anchor the dream into a context central to the interpretation.

A sub-focus often appears as an exaggerated element in a dream. Someone's nose is ridiculously large. The gun fired but shot water that didn't reach the target. Someone reaches out in friendship, but their hands are enormous. Words lift off a page in 3D, like a pop-up book.

Details

Details in a dream add even more clues for the overall message. Details involve where, when, and what else was part of the dream.

Where does it take place - My house? My childhood home? Someone else's house? A vehicle? A building? A town square? Nature? A city or the countryside? Underwater? In space?

When does the dream take place - What time-period is the setting? Is it current day but the characters are the age they were years ago? Is the dream set hundreds of years in the past? Does it take place in the future?

What else is in the dream? Animals, vehicles, weather events, objects, weapons, roads, clothing, prominent colors, numbers in the dream?

Title Your Dream

Once you finish recording your dream, see if you can come up with a title for the dream. Why a title? Besides challenging your creative juices and revving up your right brain, coming up with a title helps boil the dream down to its central theme. A glance at the title can quickly take you back into the "movie" of the dream. Months or years later, when you are reviewing your dreams, instead of reading through a dream until your mind clicks into that particular night parable, seeing the title can engage your spirit right away.

Category

After giving it a title, ask the Lord to help you determine the category of the dream. Is this a calling dream? A correction dream? Is it a dream the Lord gave to help you empathize more fully with others struggling with circumstances you haven't experienced? Is it a soul dream? A flushing dream? Determining a category provides a solid framework as you process.

Diagramming a dream is one of the most effective ways of seeing the big picture of your dream while not losing sight of the details. Here's an example of how I diagrammed one of my most significant dreams:

Dream:

> I walk into a café. The café consists of a big open room with a long table with benches directly in front of me. Everything in the café is yellow. The table is yellow, the walls are yellow, and the ceiling is yellow. I am standing at one end of the table and sitting at the opposite end is my beautiful cousin who has been estranged from me for a number of years. I am surprised to see her and feel uncertain how to act. She smiles exuberantly, jumps up and runs toward me. We meet in the middle, and

she hugs me. She says, "What are you doing here?" I replied, "I know the owner." She enthusiastically says, "I know the owner, too!" Just then the owner comes through the curtained door that leads to the kitchen and enters the room.

Date _____ Title: <u>Joyful Reconciliation!</u>

INTERPRETATION:

The Lord is communicating hope (yellow typically represents hope) to the dreamer that this estranged relationship will be restored. The dreamer and their cousin both share a love for the Lord (the Owner) and feed on the same spiritual nourishment. They're no longer at opposite ends of the table but are reunited. The table has room for many more, and this reconciliation will bring great joy.

The Lord gave me this dream — remember, only God knows the future —about four years before this beautiful reconciliation took place in the natural.

You may be thinking, "All this info on recording dreams is great, but what do you do if you forget your dreams?" Ask the Holy Spirit to help you remember. I know, I know. It sounds simple. But just asking before you sleep to remember your dreams—or as soon as you wake up—is surprisingly effective. It sets your intention, and God honors that.[40]

> Diagramming a dream is one of the most effective ways of seeing the big picture of your dream while not losing sight of the details.

Another tip for remembering is to go back and lay down in the spot where you had the dream. This has worked for me a number of times. In fact, if I've had a busy day and didn't make the bed in the morning, I often find myself slipping right back into the last dream scenario when I get in at night. So, to create a clean slate for my dreams, I'll make the bed before hopping in. It's like preparing my space to receive something fresh.

Although somewhat daunting at first, the habit of remembering and recording your dreams will produce valuable fruit in your life. I can promise you that, not only from personal experience, but because when we value what God values, He gives us more. So, before you sleep tonight, ask God for dreams and the ability to remember them. I suggest taking an action that shows faithful expectation—like placing a notebook and pen, or your phone, next to your bed so you're ready to capture your dreams as soon as you wake.

REFLECTIONS

1. How do you currently approach recording your dreams? After reading the various methods suggested in the chapter (voice notes, writing, diagrams, etc.), which method resonates with you the most? Why?

_____

_____

_____

2. What is your experience with recurring people, places, or symbols in your dreams?

_____

_____

_____

3. Reflect on a recent dream you've had. What do you think the main focus of the dream was? Were there any recurring symbols, people, or settings that stood out to you? How might these relate to your current life or journey with God?

_____

_____

_____

4. What challenges do you face when trying to remember and record your dreams?

_____

_____

_____

5. How does the practice of recording dreams align with the idea of "faithfulness in little things"? (Luke 16:10)

_____

_____

_____

Chapter 8

EVALUATING A DREAM

A dream from God may not always line up with my current understanding, but it will always align with the character of God.

Dream:

> I was trying to find a parking spot for my high school graduation. No spots were left in the school parking lot, so I parked across the street in a small auto mechanic parking lot. I was dressed in a nice skirt, heels and an elegant blouse. I walked into the large auditorium and the rest of the graduates were on the stage for a dress rehearsal. I was shocked to see that every graduate was wearing jeans and a red t-shirt. I felt embarrassed that I was dressed differently and that I hadn't gotten the memo on the dress code change.

Our take on a dream can tell us a lot about how we perceive God, how we view ourselves, and how we understand the world around us. That in itself is an incredible gift.

When I first started processing dreams with the Holy Spirit, my default mode was to interpret my dreams through the single lens that

God was trying to show me where I was wrong. I still hadn't shaken the belief that the Father's main focus was to change me into a better version of myself.

For the record, if you were to ask me, I would have told you I didn't see God that way at all. I was sure I saw my relationship with the Father free from demands to improve. You know, through the lens of Romans 8:1, *"There is therefore now no condemnation for those who are in Christ Jesus."* At least, that's what I thought in my head. My heart told a different story.

It was only a few years into studying dream interpretation that I had the dream above. Upon waking, I was not a happy camper. I felt a wave of condemnation. My interpretation was that I, once again, was out of step and did not understand what to do. "When will I ever get it right?" I thought. "And why was I back in high school again? Why is it so hard for me to learn what I need to? What was wrong with me?"

Even as I write this, I can still feel a twinge—remembering how unkind I was to myself. Unfortunately, I didn't yet grasp the kindness and nearness of our good Father.

Discouraged, I decided once again to reach out to my dear friend, Lori, who was further down this road of understanding dreams. I told her my dream and my conclusions. Her response took me by surprise.

> *Our take on a dream can tell us a lot about how we perceive God, how we view ourselves, and how we understand the world around us.*

> *"I think this is an encouraging dream. In the dream you did graduate, and you were dressed more professionally than everyone else. It is just showing you that your path and how your life looks is unique, different from the majority. Repeated school dreams is just an encouragement that you are learning."*

Her positive, and I believe correct, take on the dream hadn't even crossed my mind. I neglected the sub-focuses and details and went straight for the embarrassment I *felt* in the dream. My interpretation uncovered a great deal about how I saw God and how I saw myself.

Looking back, I realize that learning dream interpretation has provided numerous opportunities to move from striving to earn God's approval into resting in His delight. Each time I mistakenly interpreted a dream as a call to "try harder," I came to the humbling realization that I had it all wrong. In those moments, I could hear the gentle whisper of the Father saying, "I'm not like that at all."

> When head knowledge is out of balance with personal encounter and relationship, it distorts God's intended expression through His image-bearers.

During the dream interpretation courses I was taking in that season, from time to time, I would approach John Paul Jackson with a dream. After telling the dream, before he could even respond, I'd often blurt out, "That's bad, isn't it?" With a bright smile and a twinkle in his eyes, he would say, "No, it's good! That's a *good* dream!" This so impacted me that as we began developing our dream community in 2017, I was teased for repeatedly saying, "No, this is a *good* dream!"

After all, every dream *is* an invitation to connect with God.

With all of this in mind, let's dive into the practical steps of processing a dream.

Pray As You Process

You have your dream recorded, and you've identified the focus, sub-focuses, and details. Now, it's time to partner with God as you process. Remember - only the Lord knows the interpretation of a dream. Dialogue with the Holy Spirit as you sort through it.

Suspend Logic and Judgment and Keep an Open Mind

I once had a dream where I encountered an individual I had trouble recognizing, although I knew this person was in a ministry leadership position. I couldn't make out who he was because his bald head was so swollen that his facial features were almost completely obscured. As I prayed over the dream, the message became clear: When head knowledge is out of balance with personal encounter and relationship, it distorts God's intended expression through His image-bearers.

As we discussed earlier, in Western culture, we tend to rely heavily on reasoning and intellect. Our go-to approach is often to process things through left-brain functions. But dreams aren't meant to be clear. They are enigmas, dark sayings, and metaphors. They are designed to captivate us, in the best possible way, prompting us to seek God for understanding. And from that relational experience, our spirit receives both understanding and strength, drawn from the joy of being in His Presence.

Dreams have layers of interpretation, and we may not always get the full understanding right away. It could take years to fully grasp their meaning. And then, one day, we'll have that moment of clarity— "Oh, this was that!"

Lisa, my co-author for my previous book, *Light in our Darkness*, had a dream four years ago that was brief and had clear imagery. She thought maybe it was related to her family destiny, but that context for interpretation didn't quite "land." Recently on our prayer call, four years later, the Lord revealed the mystery of the dream. It turns out the dream was for the country, and we can clearly see it unfolding today.

> Dreams aren't meant to be clear. They are enigmas, dark sayings, and metaphors.

As you evaluate a dream, do your best to suspend logic and judgment. This is not an intellectual pursuit. This process is a partnership with the Holy Spirit to comprehend His metaphorical language. Pay close attention to any preconceived opinions, as they can mute the true meaning of a dream. Our own reactions and insecurities can carry over into the dream, but they may not reflect the actual message or parable being communicated.

Approach each dream with an open mind and an engaged right brain. This is a beautiful invitation to ask the Holy Spirit to help us open our hearts to a greater understanding of His ways and His perspective.

Stay True To The Dream

While tethered to ongoing communion with the Holy Spirit and maintaining an open mind, one of the most essential principles is to stay true to the dream. I feel so strongly about this that the very first post on my dream social media accounts addressed this. If we insert our current circumstances, personal passions, or focus into the interpretation process, they can easily steer us away from the true message.

I recently experienced this when a dream was shared at a dream interpretation seminar.

> *"In my dream, I was in my house and walked into the living room. I was dismayed to see multiple workers outside dismantling the bricks of my back wall, tearing it down. I turned around to see the same thing happening to the front of my house!"*

After sharing the dream, this individual quickly followed up explaining that they had recently become aware of the weakening of our national borders in America and felt that the dream was about the country.

As always, I began by repeating the dream back to the dreamer, asking a few clarifying questions. Then I responded,

> *"I believe this dream is about you and your life. It's what we call a current condition dream. The dream indicates*

that there are personal boundaries that are being torn down by outside influences. It is rightfully distressing to you. The Lord is inviting you to come to Him to look at this dynamic and partner with Him to rebuild and secure those appropriate boundaries."

The dreamer immediately resonated with this interpretation as an "aha" lightbulb went off in their spirit. I went on to explain,

*"We have to stay true to the dream. Although this dream may have similarities to what you've been discovering about the country, the dream takes place in **your** house. Your house represents your life. It didn't take place at the capitol or at a national border, for instance. In addition, there are no other people present. Only the strangers outside who are dismantling your walls. For these reasons, the dream is about you."*

The dreamer had been imposing a current focus onto the dream, which resulted in a diversion from the true meaning. In reality, it was much more intimate; a message from the Lord's heart about their personal well-being.

Another facet of staying true to the dream is to be rigorously honest with yourself. This is something that takes vigilance and courage. Don't embellish, don't eliminate. The wrong interpretation because of an unwillingness to be fully honest can lead to self-pity, resentment, manipulation, and even delay our destiny. In the long run, it's not worth it.

Reduce the Dream to its Simplest Form

When you finish processing a dream, you should be able to tell the message of the dream in a couple of sentences. In other words, the goal is to reduce the dream to its simplest form. I have found this to be one of the most challenging skills to master in dream interpretation. Dreams, after all, can be epic sagas with multiple scenes and countless details. Or they can be a cryptic one scene scenario. Either way, it's helpful to be able to state the message simply.

Here are a few examples.

Dream:

> *"I dreamed that alligators were coming after me and I was running to get away from them. These alligators were a group of people I knew personally. There was one friend that was half-alligator from the waist down and human from the waist up. This half alligator was also being chased by the other alligators."*

Interpretation:

> *"This dream is about you, the dreamer. God is warning you to be cautious about being vulnerable with influential people who verbally attack and slander. Your friend is in the process of transformation and is also working to distance themselves from this negative influence. They have yet to get free of being negatively influenced by the lies."*

Alligator: someone with influence, slandering and circulating lies with the goal of taking another person down (powerful mouth, strong tail – "tale," destroys).

Dream:

My friend's cryptic dream –
> *"In this dream I was somewhere with food."*

Interpretation:

> *"God is encouraging you that no matter where you are, your spiritual and physical needs will be met."*

Dream:

> *"I dreamed that I was in a college classroom, and it was final exam day. I had not been to class all semester. I felt panicked. Just then, the professor walked over to me and told me he was going to help me with the test. In the dream, I was relieved. I was surprised and thankful that I would have help. I knew I would pass the test."*

Interpretation:

> *"This dream is about you, the dreamer. God is letting you know you are in a time of testing, and although you feel unprepared, He will help you through it, and you'll pass the test if you partner with Him."*

Dream:

> *"I dreamed that I'm back in school."*

Interpretation:

> *"God is revealing that you are in a season of learning."*

The details of the dream inform what kind of learning it is. Was the setting in college? Then, the dreamer is in a season of learning to gain a higher level of understanding. Were they in elementary school? The dreamer is in a time of learning elementary or foundational things. "Back in school" dreams are great dreams to have. It could be that God is reinforcing something He's taught before or perhaps something not quite mastered the first time around.

When evaluating a dream, the big picture summary is what we're aiming for. To get there, here are some helpful steps to guide you in uncovering the true message of the dream.

Read or Tell the Dream Out Loud

It's remarkable what will jump out as we read the dream out loud. Once, I had a dream in which I looked down and noticed that I had a few sores on my thigh that looked like worms under my skin. In the dream, I thought to myself, "Well, that's not good!" (Have you ever noticed that God doesn't seem to mind offending our senses in dreams?)

When I was re-telling this dream to a friend, as soon as I heard the phrase "under my skin," it suddenly clicked for me. I knew that I had allowed some comments directed at me to get under my skin. From my natural perspective, I was convinced that those words had no effect on me. But the dream showed that my reaction to the things that were said were eating away at my "walk in life" (my legs). I confessed this to my friend, repented on the spot for holding onto resentment, and asked the Lord to wash me clean.[41]

"Why THIS and not THAT?"

One of the most effective tools John Paul Jackson emphasized in reviewing a dream is asking, "Why this and not that?" This simple exercise has proven to be incredibly helpful in evaluating the context of the dream. It's amazing how this question can bring clarity to elements that might otherwise be overlooked or undervalued.

Why were we in my childhood home and not in an office building? Why was I driving a red sports car and not a school bus?

Why was I in an airport terminal and not on a plane?

Why was his nose exaggerated in the dream and not his ears?

Why was it a bear and not a tiger?

Why was I yelling and not speaking calmly?

Why was everyone wearing clothes from the 1970s and not current day attire?

Why was the dream set at night and not in broad daylight?

You get the picture. Simply asking "why this and not that" brings features of the dream into sharper focus. The significance of the particulars informs a more wholistic meaning.

Think Symbolically, Not Literally

Looking at the elements of the dream, again, evaluate symbolically not literally. God specifically crafts a dream to deliver a message to the dreamer. Watch for puns, parables, metaphors, similes, homonyms, idioms, exaggerations, etc. The Bible is chock-full of these literary devices. (More on that in Chapter 9).

God's first recorded word to Jeremiah employed a homonym. God loves a good play on words.

> *"The word of the LORD came to me: 'What do you see, Jeremiah?'*
> *'I see the branch of an almond tree,' I replied. The LORD said to me,*
> *'You have seen correctly for I am watching to see that my word is fulfilled.'"*
> ~ Jeremiah 1:11-12

Huh? To our non-Hebrew ears, this makes no sense at all. What in the world does an almond branch have to do with God watching over His word to fulfill it? But to the Hebrew listener, they would immediately recognize it as a play on words, or a homonym:

Hebrew word *Shaqed* =almond tree

Hebrew word *Shaqad* = watchful

These words sound the same and convey an image (almond tree) to go along with the concept of the message (God is watching).

Speaking of trees, *people* are often symbolically referred to as *trees*:

"He shall be like a tree planted by living waters."
~ Psalm 1:3

"They shall be called Oaks of righteousness."
~ Isaiah 61:3

In Nebuchadnezzar's dream, the tree represented him.

"Your Majesty, you are that tree."
~ Daniel 4:22

Jesus, in addition to His fondness for parables, loved communicating in metaphors. A metaphor is a figure of speech in which a word or phrase is representative or symbolic of something else. For example: "He's a night owl" or "That's the icing on the cake." Jesus' seven "I am" statements in the Gospel of John are perfect examples of God's use of metaphors in the Scriptures.

> Dream interpretation tools can be helpful but are *always* secondary to the Word of God.

"I am the bread of life" (John 6:35).
"I am the light of the world" (John 8:12).
"I am the door" (John 10:7).
"I am the good shepherd" (John 10:11, 14).
"I am the resurrection and the life" (John 11:25).
"I am the way the truth and the life" (John 14:6).
"I am the true vine" (John 15:1).

Ask the Holy Spirit for Scriptures
that Apply to the Dream

This is an ideal time to return to a key foundational principle. The Word of God and its principles outweigh any other resource at our disposal. Dream interpretation tools can be helpful but are *always* secondary to the Word of God. As you are working through a dream, keep your Bible handy and search the Word for passages that speak to a given scenario. Trees, water, bread, wine, seeds, soil, and storms are all biblical themes. And so much more. The exodus is riddled with God revealing His character through imagery. The poetry of the Psalms, Proverbs and Song of Solomon spill over with the language of metaphors, idioms, and similes.

> Ask God to show you the Scriptures through fresh eyes of wonder.

Read and listen to the Word! Devour it! Ask the Holy Spirit for greater understanding and you will see your ability to think metaphorically soar. Ask God to show you the Scriptures through fresh eyes of wonder. Ask questions and keep asking. How did Jesus use these themes to teach kingdom realities?

The brilliant Yo-Yo Ma recently released a book centered around the idea of approaching everything with the mindset of a beginner. I love this. Isn't that what Jesus emphasized when telling us we must be like a child to enter the Kingdom way of life?[42]

Process Your Dream with Others

One of the best resources we have in evaluating dreams is other believers. However, it's crucial to exercise good judgment when deciding who to share these personal experiences with. A mutual understanding of dreams and the protocol with which we handle them is vital. I'll talk about some of the ground rules for this more extensively in Chapter 18, which talks about community.

In my circles, sending dreams to one another and asking for prayerful insight is a regular occurrence. I frequently rely on our community of dreamers to help me understand my own dreams. They are incredibly helpful in pointing out aspects I've overlooked or construed to my preconceived mindset.

The reality is, often we are "too close" to our dreams to look at them objectively. Others can more readily pick up on context and details we miss. They frequently perceive things in our dreams which we are unknowingly resistant or even blind to. I believe we will find that a brother or sister will extend us grace – perhaps grace that we are neglecting to give to ourselves!

To wrap it up: when you're working through a dream, stay connected to the Holy Spirit. Let yourself shift into right-brain mode—where creativity, curiosity, and discernment live. This isn't the time for logic and judgment to drive; instead, let metaphorical thinking take the wheel. Focus on what actually showed up in the dream and try not to project your own assumptions onto it. Use tools like asking, "Why this and not that?" while telling the dream out loud and inviting someone else into the process to help unpack it. And always—always—filter everything through the Word of God.

> Often, we are "too close" to our dreams to look at them objectively.

REFLECTIONS

1. Does the idea of approaching dreams symbolically rather than literally challenge you? Why or why not?

_____

_____

_____

2. How does reducing the dream to its simplest form help in the interpretation process?

_____

_____

_____

3. What concepts presented were new to you in evaluating a dream?

_____

_____

_____

4. What are some practical ways to hold up your dream to the light of Scripture?

_____

_____

_____

5. How can you ensure that you stay true to the message of your dreams, without letting your personal circumstances or biases influence the interpretation?

_____

_____

_____

Chapter 9

PROCESSING METAPHORICALLY

"The most powerful tool to learn metaphors is the Bible."
~ John Paul Jackson

In this chapter, we'll take a brief look at the literary devices that God uses in Scripture, as well as how He still communicates today. The Scriptures are rich with imagery, word plays, and parables. He even had His prophets live out metaphors with their own lives to get His message across. It truly is the primary language of God. Abundance of wine, for instance, is a metaphor for abundant joy; honey a symbol for the Word of God; apples of gold set in silver is a metaphor for timely wise words.

"You have put more joy in my heart than they have
when their grain and wine abound."
~ Psalm 4:7

"How sweet are your words to my taste, sweeter than honey to my mouth!"
~ Psalm 119:103

> *"A word fitly spoken is like apples of gold in settings of silver."*
> ~ Proverbs 25:11

In the same way, there are symbolic elements in dreams, and as dream interpreters with a biblical lens, we have a baseline for what some of those things represent. However, God knows us so intimately that He uses metaphors and symbols unique and special to us; tailor made dream communication for each person. Like our own private movie theater.

A friend of mine shared a dream she had about whales, and in the dream, one swam up to her and hovered right beside her. Whales typically represent someone who dives deep into the spiritual realm, especially the Holy Spirit, or someone with significant influence. But for my friend, whales are special. They are her favorite mammal due to their size, their grace, and because their brains are wired for social connection. They remind her of the majesty, authority, and nearness of God. And the Lord knows that. So, when God gave her this whale dream, the whale symbolized the awe-inspiring experience of God's presence when He draws near to her. Isn't that beautiful?

Literary Devices Used by the Lord

Metaphor

A metaphor is a figure of speech in which a word or phrase is applied to an object or action to which it is not literally applicable. For example: "I had fallen through a trap door of addiction." It's representative or symbolic of something else. David employs the use of metaphor in describing the word of God as a light.

> *"Your word is a lamp to my feet, and a light to my path."*
> ~ Psalm 119:105

Simile

A simile describes an experience or object by comparing it to a different experience or object. They include a comparison word such as *like* or *as*. Similes are used to make a description more emphatic or vivid. For instance, "as brave as a lion" or "dumb like a fox." An iconic Scripture example of this is David's:

"As the deer pants for streams of water, so my soul pants for you, my God."
~ Psalm 42:1

Homophone

Words that sound the same but are spelled differently, otherwise known as a play on words. A great biblical example of a homophone is the Lord's creation of Adam.

"Then the LORD God formed man (adam) *from the dust of the ground* (adamah)*..."*
The word for human (adam), reflects his origin, ground/earth (adamah).

Idiom

A phrase or expression that has a figurative meaning different from the literal meaning of the individual words. For instance, "Spill the beans" means to reveal a secret, not to pour out a can of beans. A Scriptural example found in Isaiah uses the idiom "A drop in the bucket," meaning a very small, insignificant amount.

"Surely the nations are like a drop in a bucket; they are regarded as dust on the scales; he weighs the islands as though they were fine dust."
~ Isaiah 40:15

Allegory

A story, poem, or picture that can be interpreted to reveal a hidden meaning. An allegory is a story, poem, or picture in which the characters and/or events are symbols representing other events, ideas, or people. One of the most famous allegories in Scripture is the story of *The Prodigal Son* found in Luke 15:11-32, describing our waywardness and the love of our Heavenly Father toward those who have wandered from the faith.

Hyperbole

Hyperbole is the use of exaggeration, overstatement, or magnification to stress a point. Have you ever heard a kid say, "Mom, what's for dinner? I'm *starving!*" In Scripture, David uses hyperbole:

> *"I am weary with my moaning; every night I flood my bed*
> *with tears; I drench my couch with my weeping."*
> ~ Psalm 6:6

Jesus also employed hyperbole to get his point across:

> *"If your right eye causes you to stumble, gouge it out and throw it away."*
> ~ Matthew 5:29-30

Symbols

A symbol is a thing that represents or stands for something else, especially a material object representing something abstract. For example: "The limousine was another emblem of his position in wealth." In the Bible, Jesus used symbolism in the last Supper.

> *"...took the bread...this is my body which is broken for you...*
> *He took the cup...this cup is the new covenant in my blood."*
> ~ 1 Corinthians 11:23-26

Analogies

An analogy is something that shows how two things are alike, but with the ultimate goal of making a point about this comparison. The purpose of an analogy is not merely to show, but also to explain. "Unforgiveness is like drinking poison expecting the other person to die." A biblical example:

"Go to the ant, you sluggard! Consider her ways and be wise."
~ Proverbs 6:6

Parables

A parable is a simple story used to illustrate a moral or spiritual lesson. They may have several facets but only one central point. For example, Jesus tells the parable of the sower and the seed.

"Then he told them many things in parables, saying:
'A farmer went out to sow his seed...'"
~ Matthew 13:1-23

The story contains many elements but with one focus – the condition of the soil of the heart determines the fruit of the word of God in a life.

The literary devices we see in Scripture aren't just creative flourishes—they're techniques God uses to communicate deep truths in ways we can understand. Whether it's through metaphors, parables, or symbols, these tools help paint a clearer picture of God's heart, His kingdom, and our relationship with Him. They help us to grasp the unseen realm and God's principles in ways that resonate with our human experience. God continues to speak to us through imagery and stories to draw us closer to Him. When we learn to perceive a message through the lens of these literary concepts, whether in Scripture or a dream, we not only get a better sense of how He's revealed Himself in the past but also how He is speaking to us right now.

REFLECTIONS

1. What are some examples in your life where a metaphor or symbol has helped you better understand God's guidance or presence?

_____

_____

_____

2. Why do you think God uses so many different literary devices (like parables, analogies, and hyperbole) to communicate with us? What does that say about His desire for connection?

_____

_____

_____

3. Do you see modern culture using metaphors or symbols in a similar way to how the Bible does? How might noticing these in everyday life help you to look at dreams metaphorically?

_____

_____

_____

4. How does God's use of literary devices like metaphors and parables make His messages more relatable to us?

_____

_____

_____

5. How can the knowledge of biblical metaphors enhance our understanding of God's language in everyday life or in dreams?

_____

_____

_____

Chapter 10

STEWARDING DREAMS FOR ME (INTRINSIC DREAMS)

Dream:

> *"Sometime in 2018, I had a dream in which I knew I needed to stock up on toilet paper and paper towels. But especially TP."*

Dismissing directives in our dreams could leave us high and dry for what is ahead. When I had this dream, we had been setting aside food and "essential needs" in case of emergency for the past 10 years. So, I was surprised to wake up from this dream knowing the clear message was to order extra toilet paper. I mean, we already *had* extra TP. But because of the dream, I went online again and ordered several large boxes, along with a big supply of paper towels. And there they sat. Staring at me every time I went into our attic.

I'll be honest. I began to feel a little silly as

An intrinsic dream is a dream for and about the dreamer.

months and months went by with no apparent need for the ridiculous amount of TP and paper towels. I began to think that maybe I was mistaken or didn't interpret the dream correctly.

And then the COVID-19 pandemic hit the nation, along with the ubiquitous shortage of toilet paper. We had plenty for ourselves, several of our sons who moved in temporarily, and to share with anyone who got caught in the shortage. You know, God really does take care of His kids. He is in the details.

Intrinsic Dreams

An intrinsic dream is a dream for and about the dreamer. Obviously, not every intrinsic dream has such a practical application. Many times, as the dreamer, an intrinsic dream can seem inconsequential, or chaotic and confusing. The temptation is to label the dream as "too weird" or "it makes no sense" and discard it. However, it's remarkable how many of our "crazy" or "throwaway" dreams take on meaning when we muse on them with the Holy Spirit or in the company of others. Often, something in the natural,[43] even months down the road, can rivet the dream into sharp focus, and the enigma of the dream becomes clear.

Most dreams from God are to instruct and encourage us. The mystery of a dream is our Father's invitation to engage in a conversation and gain deeper understanding. It's all about relationship. Frequently our dreams are related to our current assignment, whether a job, our family, a current undertaking, or our community. Once our assignment shifts, so do our dreams.

God's communication with us in dreams often matures as we mature. Joseph's dreams at the beginning of his life were all about him – his destiny and calling. Near the end of his life, God praised him for having the vision to ask that his bones be brought back to the promised land—showing he truly understood the bigger picture.[44] He encouraged his brothers about *their* destiny and the destiny of their tribes – God *would* take them from Egypt and bring them back to the land of promise.[45]

Remembering that the Lord Himself places such high value on dreams, one of the first principles when we receive dreams is to thank Him and determine to honor them as a gift. We posture our hearts to value what he values.

Determine to Obey What God Shows Us in a Dream

"Teach me Your way, O Lord; I will walk in Your
truth; Unite my heart to fear Your name."
~ Psalm 86:11

"I have inclined my heart to perform Your statutes forever, even to the end."
~ Psalm 119:112

"The LORD is my portion; I have promised to keep Your words."
~ Psalm 119:57

Above all, make every effort to approach your dreams with an open and willing mindset. A heart that is positioned to obey is an invitation for God to reveal more of Himself to us.

"The one who has My commandments and keeps them is the one
who loves Me; and the one who loves Me will be loved by My
*Father, and I will love him and **will reveal Myself** to him."*
~ John 14:21

What if, in a dream, the Lord warns us not to speak about something? Maybe it's a topic we *really* want to address with someone. Or, conversely, a dream indicates that we need to talk through an issue with someone, and we're reluctant. What if God shows us through a dream that a relationship we cherish isn't the healthiest choice? What if

God reveals a calling on our life, and instead of feeling excited, we're overwhelmed and, like Jonah, want to run the other way?

The question is, are we willing to *obey* when the message conflicts with what we want? Will our current understanding trump the message of the dream? I encourage you to simply pray and tell the Father that you are willing to receive and obey what He wants to reveal. Then invite the Lord to give you dreams. It's amazing how generous He is when He's invited.

Ask the Lord to Reveal Hidden Things in your Heart

"Search me, God, and know my heart; test me
and know my anxious thoughts.
See if there is any offensive way in me and lead me in the way everlasting."
~ Psalm 139:23, 24

> Are we willing to *obey* when the message conflicts with what we want?

Dreams are one of the most effective ways for the Holy Spirit to show us destructive issues and attitudes that are hidden from our conscious minds. Our defenses are down, and we are the more receptive to God's communication. The Father loves us so much that He longs to make the crooked ways straight in our lives. We all have "ways" of viewing Him, ourselves and the world that don't align with His character and beautiful design; we have counterproductive patterns that delay our God-given destiny and ways that withhold our contribution from others. Ways that defer hope and sicken our hearts.

Pray Psalm 139:23, 24, telling the Lord that you want Him to show you hidden things, and be sure to thank Him when He does.

Process Through the Lens of Scripture

"All Scripture is God-breathed and is useful for teaching, rebuking,
correcting and training in righteousness, so that the servant of
God may be thoroughly equipped for every good work."
~ 2 Timothy 3:16-17

Ask the Holy Spirit to bring Scripture and Kingdom principles to mind as you mull the dream over with Him. Dreams are night parables and, many times, elements in our dreams are found in the Bible. In fact, many of the dream elements we rely on in interpretation are taken directly from Scripture, which happens to be jam-packed with symbolism. It goes without saying that messages from the Lord reflect principles found in Scripture.

> Dreams are one of the most effective ways for the Holy Spirit to show us destructive issues and attitudes that are hidden from our conscious minds.

Once again, the more you read and meditate on Scripture, the more you will understand the language of God in your dreams. And knowing His language brings joy.

"Your words were found, and I ate them, and Your word
was to me the joy and rejoicing of my heart, for I am
called by Your name, O Lord God of Hosts."
~ Jeremiah 15:16

Process With Others

"Listen to counsel and receive instruction, that you may be
wise in your latter days. There are many plans in a man's
heart, nevertheless the Lord's counsel—that will stand."
~ Proverbs 19:20-21

In Chapter 8, we talked about how one of best things we can do when evaluating dreams is to lean on the insight of other believers. In the West, we often place a strong emphasis on individualism, which in and of itself isn't bad. But figuring it out on our own can make us more susceptible to deception and prevent us from experiencing the powerful synergy that comes from connecting with others. The Scriptures reveal that we have exponential, supernatural strength in numbers.

"Five of you shall chase a hundred, and a hundred
of you shall put ten thousand to flight…"
~ Leviticus 26:8

The nature of dreams is that they can elicit a full range of emotions, and often exaggerated emotion. When we wake from a dream, we've just been through a whole multidimensional experience. It often includes unfamiliar settings, intense feelings, and our minds working to make sense of the people, events, and interactions we encounter.

> Frequently we are not the most objective with our own dreams.

I want to re-emphasize that frequently we are not the most objective with our own dreams. We miss major details. We carry our personal filter into our evaluation. We gloss over elements that conflict with our preconceived perspectives. Confirmation bias can selectively craft our understanding, muting or distorting the message. By ourselves it is more challenging to "stay true to the dream."

It's just plain wisdom to get counsel from mature believers who understand dreams. They can often pick up on things we overlook and tend to be more gracious with us than we are with ourselves. This is especially true if we have a dream community that follows the proper protocol and operates in the fruit of the Spirit. (More on that in Chapter 13.)

Declare any Promises God Gives in a Dream

We're already familiar with claiming the promises in God's Word for our lives. But do you know that if the Lord reveals direction or a promise through a dream, we can also hold onto that and declare it as His truth for us? This is in line with the concept of a *rhema* word from God.

Dreams that carry the fingerprints of heaven contain prophetic seeds - seeds of promise. Joseph was given two dreams foretelling his future position of authority over his family. The fact that he had two dreams confirmed the certainty of the message; a principle years later he related to Pharoah about Pharoah's two dreams.[46] Joseph's dreams certainly didn't manifest immediately. In fact, they seemed more and more impossible with each devastating turn of events. Personally, I believe the dreams kept him going as year after year dragged on, feeding him hope in his darkest days.

> Dreams that carry the fingerprints of heaven contain prophetic seeds - seeds of promise.

When we receive a dream that contains a promise from God, we can agree with heaven and state it out loud! Our spoken words have incredible power. God *spoke* and the world came into being. As imagers of the Father, He has given us power in our words to release on earth what He reveals.

"Death and life are in the power of the tongue..."
~ Proverbs 18:21

All of us have found ourselves at one time or another in circumstances that are challenging or even heartbreaking. How many times have we heard ourselves verbally lamenting our current situation or a condition of someone we love? Or a church, a job, a system, city, or nation? When we receive a dream that indicates the good plans of God, we have the full go-ahead to agree with heaven as we speak it out as a certainty. I have learned to say out loud,

"The Lord has declared _____, and I agree with the plans of heaven. Let it be on earth as it is in heaven!"

We then have full confidence to rejoice and celebrate what the Lord will do.

Sometimes what the Lord promises in a dream seems too good to be true. Everything in our current circumstances appears to contradict what He showed us in a dream. *"Faith comes by hearing, and hearing by the word of God,"* Paul wrote in Romans 10:17. Once again, here the Hebrew for "word" is not logos but *rhema*. Remember, *rhema* is an utterance of God, a present time "word" from God. A dream from God is a present time utterance, a revelation from heaven. As we speak out the promise in a dream, we hear it, and our faith increases to believe it.

Many parents are praying for their grown prodigal children to return to the Lord. In our community, we've received dreams that promise the restoration of our beloved prodigals, and we've declared that the Lord is faithfully fulfilling these promises. As I write, we are witnessing these precious ones take steps toward or even running toward home.

> A dream from God is a present time utterance, a revelation from heaven.

When I had the dream that promised reconciliation with my beautiful cousin, long before it happened in the natural, I shared it with others. Together, we spoke out in faith, declaring that it would come to pass because the Lord said so. And it did.

Many have received dreams with strategy for healing in their friendships, marriages, or in parenting their kids. As they have thanked the Lord for these gifts of dreams and followed through, Jesus, the Great Reconciler, has navigated them into flourishing relationships.

Review and Pray Over your Dreams

Have you ever noticed how often the Scriptures urge us to "remember"? Every now and then, you might find yourself, like I do, caught up in the chaos of life, feeling a bit lost or uncertain about your purpose. Sensing you're a little adrift, needing to anchor yourself in the steadying presence of God. Just to be reassured by His Truth, calmed by His Love, or just refreshed with a new perspective from His Kingdom.

If so, it's no wonder. We are bombarded with distractions. The media aims to define us and occupy our thoughts with their priorities. The responsibilities of everyday life and those around us vie for our attention. Disappointment in ourselves and disappointments with others drain us of joy. Fear of the future and regrets over the past plague us. The list goes on and on.

One of the surest ways to anchor into the reassurance and comforting direction of God is to *remember*. Remember all He has done in our lives. Remember all He's done in Scripture and historically. Remember His promises. Remember what He's done for the people around us. Remember specific promises He's made to us.

Remembering emphasizes His love and hosts His reassuring Presence. In that space He quiets the noise, helping to reorient us back to His sweeping narrative and the unique role we play in it.

One aspect of this practice of "remembering" involves reflecting on and revisiting our dreams. Reading through our past dreams brings fresh recollection of what God has already fulfilled. It reminds us of promises to claim and to declare what has yet to manifest. A correction through a dream as to how we conduct ourselves comes into renewed focus. Forgotten actions to take and people the Father has nudged us to pray for reemerge on our list of priorities. Hopeful messages from His heart to ours recharges our batteries.

I encourage you to set aside time periodically to re-read (or listen to) your dreams. Schedule an hour or an afternoon alone with the Lord to review and reflect on these night parables. Ask for clarity. Ask for more insight into different elements. Enjoy a laugh with Him about the comical details. Take time to thank Him for connecting with you in this way. I'm confident you'll be glad you did, and I know the Lord will deeply treasure that time with you.

Intrinsic dreams are such a gift from the Lord. They might appear random or unimportant at times but it's remarkable how often they hold deeper meaning when we invite the Holy Spirit to help us interpret them. Each dream is an opportunity to draw nearer to Him and understand more of His heart. Keep honoring and reflecting on the dreams He shares with you. Allow the One who cares deeply about every part of your life to draw you a little closer through His night parables, crafted just for you. I think you'll be glad you did.

REFLECTIONS

1. How can asking God to reveal hidden things in your heart through dreams bring clarity to areas of your life?

---

2. In what ways can you hold a dream up to the light of Scripture to understand the elements and determine if it is from God?

---

3. Are there any "crazy" or "insignificant" dreams you've had that might actually hold deeper meaning?

---

4. Have you received any dreams recently that you are hesitant to act on? Why?

_____

_____

_____

5. Are there any promises from God in your dreams that you need to declare and stand in agreement with?

_____

_____

_____

Chapter 11

STEWARDING DREAMS FOR OTHERS (EXTRINSIC DREAMS)

"Let all you do, be done in love."
~ 1 Corinthians 16:14

Dream:

> *This dream took place in one short scene. A friend is standing in my foyer next to my music room with his child standing behind him. The atmosphere is very bright and light. My friend is wearing a white tee shirt. I notice that someone has left $85 on my grand piano. I ask him if the money is his? (Presumably tuition for piano lessons.) He nods and instead of verbally responding, he starts reaching for his wallet to show me his ID. I laugh and reach over to touch his arm and say, "I know who you are!" As I squeeze his arm, I'm surprised to feel that he has no muscle tone. (He is very fit in the natural.) I then notice that his face is breaking out, almost as if something*

toxic beneath the surface is starting to show itself. He doesn't speak throughout this entire scene. End of dream.

How we present a dream to others is almost as important as understanding the interpretation from the Holy Spirit. I felt strongly that this dream was from the Lord. Dave and I had a good relationship with this friend and his wife, and up to that point, I had already shared several encouraging dreams with them. We had a history of favor and trust.

I knew this dream, at the very least, released insight for how to pray. But because of the potentially negative implications, I hesitated to share it with him. I decided to call a friend skilled in dream interpretation and ask for their counsel in stewarding this dream. They made an insightful observation. In the dream my friend came to me, not the other way around.

"Why not pray for him and ask the Lord to show you if you're meant to share with him?"

So, that's exactly what I did. During an event three weeks later, I unexpectedly bumped into my friend from the dream. We were standing in the lobby catching up and I sensed an "ok" from the Holy Spirit to tell him the dream. On the spot, the Holy Spirit also inspired me to share the dream by flipping it first. This is how I approached him...

"Hey, I had a dream you were in and wonder if you'd be ok with me sharing it with you?"

"Sure!" he replied.

"Ok. What stood out to me most in the dream was the message that the Lord sees you as righteous. *(Wearing a white tee shirt.)* He made that very clear. The dream also revealed that a new beginning is unfolding in your life, and God's grace is all over it. *($85 - In Hebrew, the number 8 represents new beginnings, and the number 5 is the number for grace.)* Whatever this entails, I believe it's going to involve exercising muscles you haven't used in a long time. *(His muscles were atrophied.)* The dream indicated that this coming season is connected with the Lord showing you your true identity. *(He pulled out his ID.)* It also seemed to suggest that you may have been in a toxic environment where you felt like you didn't have a voice." *(His face was broken out and he didn't speak throughout the entire scene.)*

As I shared the interpretation of the dream, tears began to well up in my friend's eyes. When I finished, his immediate response was,

"When did you have this dream?"

"About three weeks ago," I replied.

He then went on to share that three weeks earlier, he had met with leaders in the company he helped establish. During the meeting, he expressed how, in recent years, he had been relegated to a role that didn't align with his true abilities. He explained that the environment had become toxic, and he no longer felt like he had any real influence. When he finally voiced these concerns, his colleagues were supportive and made organizational changes, giving him the freedom to focus on his true strengths.

> It is vital that we pray and ask for supernatural wisdom on how to relate a dream that is for another person.

The changes in my friend's work environment ended up being temporary, but they sparked the motivation to transition to another company, where he was offered a role with significant influence. It was encouraging to watch as my friend felt "seen" by the Lord through the dream, knowing God had given it to someone who genuinely cared for him and would pray for him. I was amazed once again by the power of a dream and how God directs His children to pray for and encourage one another.

I was also grateful that the Holy Spirit led me to share the message of the dream rather than the specific details, which, on the surface, could have seemed condemning. In this case, the dream revealed that the situation wasn't a result of my friend's actions, but rather the environment he had been placed in and the harm it had quietly done over time. Sharing the dream as it was could have easily led to unnecessary feelings of embarrassment or guilt.

It is vital to pray and ask for supernatural wisdom on how to relate a dream that is for another person.

Protocol for stewarding a dream that involves others

When you have a dream that seems to be about others, the first thing to do is ask, "God, how does this dream apply to *me*?"

Would it surprise you to learn that most dreams we have that involve other people are about the *dreamer* and not about someone else? Just because someone appears in a dream doesn't mean the dream is *about them*. One way to discern if the dream is primarily for you is to take a look at how active you are in the dream. Ask yourself, "If I take myself out of the dream, does the dream fall apart?" If it does, the dream, at least in part, concerns *you*. Are you primarily observing in the dream? Then the focus of the dream is most likely extrinsic – the people or situation.

Before concluding it's about someone else, it's helpful to ask some questions to get clarity on the focus of the dream. As we discussed in earlier chapters, because dreams are metaphorical, often the person in a dream represents something else and not themselves. In Chapter 7, we covered looking at characteristics of the individuals in your dream:

- What does their name mean, and does it shed light on the meaning of the dream?
- Who might they represent?
- A husband can represent Jesus (our Bridegroom).
- A wife can represent the church (the Bride of Christ).
- The head of a corporation or a boss could represent the company.
- A child could represent the next generation.
- A pastor could symbolize the church.
- A Christian leader could represent what they're known for – apologetics, the prophetic, evangelism, or a prayer movement.
- The parent or grandparent of an adult could represent generational issues.

Is the dream providing insight into how the dreamer relates to the situation, or is it revealing information about the situation itself, independent of the dreamer?

I have discovered a consistent pattern in my dreams that has helped me determine if the dream is about me or primarily about others. If I'm in someone else's house or workplace and mostly observing, the dream is usually about their life and circumstances. The details form the intel of how God would have me pray for them or sometimes reveal hidden things that give me wisdom in how to interact with them.

Years ago, I kept having the same dream with different variations. I'd suddenly find myself in the same house of a family we knew, and I'd be desperately trying to escape because the husband would be furious that I had intruded. Taking the dream warning to heart, I prayed for them and was cautious in how I related to him in the natural. Later, I found out that he had many hidden aspects of his life, and those destructive secrets eventually surfaced. These dreams snapped into focus as these details were made known.

> Every extrinsic dream carries with it an assignment to pray. Extrinsic dreams are given as an opportunity to view someone else's life through the lens of heaven.

More often, though, I would receive dreams where I found myself in the house of a friend, and the details I observed would provide insights on how to pray for their children or to offer personal encouragement.

Extrinsic dreams call for Intercession

Every extrinsic dream carries with it an assignment to pray. A core mission of God is to restore what is broken, bringing us back to our original purpose and destiny.[47] This restoration in each of us is not in isolation, siloed off from one another. His plan is to carry out this miraculous process in community with others. Extrinsic dreams are given as an opportunity to view someone else's life through the lens of heaven.

Because Jesus took all of the blame for our sins and there is no condemnation,[48] this insight is not a license to judge or find fault. It's an opportunity to look for the gold in others and call it out in prayer. In fact, if we find ourselves reacting in judgment or disdain, the Lord has just revealed something about our own heart. Great opportunity to look at that with Him, repent and come into alignment with His heart. Like the dream the Holy Spirit directed me to flip, even a negative scenario can be shared with encouragement. When God reveals something, we know there's power present to heal and transform. It is an invitation partner with Him to bring His Kingdom perspective and transformative power into any given situation.

If you determine that the dream is primarily about someone else or an external situation, you can be sure that there's an assignment attached to it. God never reveals anything without purpose. He entrusts us with His perspective on a person or situation to collaborate with Him in bringing His life-giving influence into what the dream represents.

In every case, *bless* the people, group or circumstances represented. I heard a message years ago explaining the breakdown of the Hebrew word for *bless*. When we bless, it doesn't mean agreeing with something or someone not currently aligned with God's purposes. The word is "*barak*," and it actually conveys the meaning to bless the destiny *written for them* by God.[49] In the Greek, the word is "eulogeo," which means to "speak well of." (Think eulogy.)

> When God reveals something, we know there's power present to heal and transform.

So even if you're given a dream where your nemesis shows up, it pleases the Lord for us to "speak well" of His intention for them. Once again, our words are powerful. Keep in mind that *"death and life are in the power of the tongue,"* and James 5:16 assures us that the effective prayer of a righteous person can accomplish much.

Remember, we are Jesus' Ekklesia, authorized to exercise spiritual authority to alter the culture to look like the Kingdom of Heaven. *Pray and declare*, releasing Kingdom life into the scenario represented in the dream. Pray in all ways you know how to pray.[50] Here are a few practical steps to take:

- Thank God for the dream and His communication to you about the person/situation.
- Acknowledge in prayer what has been revealed in the dream.
- If it's negative, flip the dream and declare God's Kingdom come, His will to be done. If the enemy wants to kill, steal, and destroy - his only three moves, then God wants the opposite: abundant life. [51]
- Declare the will of God to be done in the person, group, or situation. "Through the dream, the Lord has declared that _____, and I agree and release this on earth, in Jesus' name."
- Ask the Father to send His angels to assist.[52]
- Thank and praise God that He will provide everything needed for them to carry out His will. [53]
- In Jesus' name and by the power of His blood, disempower the plans of our defeated enemy.

Should I share the dream?

This is the tricky part. The million-dollar question. We definitely need the Holy Spirit's wisdom on whether or not we share the dream. I love this encouragement from God through King Solomon,

> *"Whoever obeys His command will come to no harm,*
> **and the wise heart knows the proper time and procedure*.*"*
> ~ Ecclesiastes 8:5

Following are a few guidelines I have found helpful.

Pray and Get Counsel Before Sharing

Get feedback from those that understand dream protocol. I am convinced that dreams are designed to be a catalyst to bring us into community. If a world class dream interpreter like Daniel counseled and collaborated with his friends, you can be sure that you and I would benefit by doing the same. Consulting with mature believers will help bring clarity to next steps with an extrinsic dream.

> *"Without consultation, plans are frustrated,*
> *But with many counselors they succeed."*
> ~ Proverbs 15:22

Examine Your Motives

Ask the Holy Spirit to search your heart and show you your *true motives.*

- Are you wanting to share the dream out of obedience to the Lord, leaving the results in His hands, or are you trying to change someone's mindset or behavior?
- Is it possible your motivation is to gain recognition?
- Are you looking for approval, or to be seen?
- Are you trying to prove your worth?

When you are in an environment that values dreams, some of these negative motives may surface. This is helpful because our goal is to interact with each other with a pure heart, and when we recognize "selfish ambition," we can repent.

> *"All a person's ways seem pure to them,*
> *but motives are weighed by the LORD."*
> ~ Proverbs 16:2

"Our purpose is to please God, not people.
He alone examines the motives of our hearts."
~ 1 Thessalonians 2:4

Take the time to wait until the Holy Spirit has revealed your true motives. I often involve someone I trust to help me sort through my intentions. I have friends who will thoughtfully challenge me and ask tough questions, helping me assess things honestly. It's better to approach someone with a clean heart, not expecting anything from them.

Do You Have Favor?

Another question to evaluate with the Lord before sharing is, "Do I have *favor* with this person?" None of us can accomplish what God has assigned to us without favor. Both His favor on us and the favor we have gained through operating in truth and love.

- How long have you known this person?
- What's your track record with them?
- Do you have a history of humility, looking out for the good of the other?
- Have you served them, encouraged them?
- Have you shown up, been there for them?
- Conversely, have you highlighted weaknesses, given unsolicited advice, or attempted to manipulate or control them?

It's worth noting that it doesn't take a supernatural gift to point out what's wrong. Our role is to pray, love, and encourage. God already has the solution for them and their situation. The voice of the Lord brings conviction, not condemnation, and always communicates hope.

If your dream is for someone in a leadership role, it's especially important to be aware of the level of favor you have with them. You may receive a profound dream, but if they don't know you, it probably won't carry much weight with them. If you do not have a personal relationship with them and you feel that the Holy Spirit is directing you to communicate the dream, it's important to go through the proper channels. Receiving a dream for them doesn't entitle you to presume direct contact with them.

> *"Through presumption comes nothing but strife…"*
> ~ Proverbs 13:10 NASB

When I was part of an intercession team, our pastor welcomed dreams and occasionally shared relevant ones with us. Our team received many dreams that helped to target our prayers more effectively for him and for the church. Many were encouraging, some warnings, some glimpses into where God was taking the church, others current condition or directional. We not only prayed over the insights within the dreams, but also carefully considered how and whether we should share them.

How, When and Where to Share?

Once you feel your motives are aligned with God's heart, and you feel released to share, ask Him for wisdom on *how, when,* and *where* to communicate the dream.

- Should you share just the message or the full details of the dream itself?
- Would it be wiser to wait for the right opportunity or to take the initiative and reach out?
- Can this be shared in an email, or would it be more effective over the phone or in person?

It doesn't take a supernatural gift to point out what's wrong. Our role is to pray, love, and encourage.

Turn The Results Over To God

Once the dream has been shared, your responsibility is completed—aside from continuing to pray, there's nothing more to do. The role of an individual with some sort of prophetic message is simply *to deliver a message*. It does not grant any authority to act on or implement the message of the dream. Just as we did nothing to receive revelation from a dream, we have nothing to do with the results. Hands off. We don't become the recipient's counselor, accountability partner, or Jr. Holy Spirit. Simply thank the Holy Spirit for entrusting you with a dream and move on.

Delivering a dream and leaving the results to God can be a real test of character. After all, experiencing the dream can be emotionally impactful. What if it's a warning dream and they choose to ignore it? What if they don't follow up with you about it? Perhaps it's for a family member, friend, or colleague, and they don't take the action you believe they should. What then?

Remember, you are being entrusted with the dream, and that alone is an honor. How you steward it can influence how much the Lord may entrust to you in the future. Have you let go of frustration or expectations of others? Again, ask the Lord to search your heart.

If we're feeling frustrated, it's a sign that we've crossed our boundaries. Paul's admonishment in Romans 14 has helped me clarify what is mine and what is not. This Scripture has prompted me to repent for delivering a dream with a heaping side-helping of expectations.

> *"But as for you, why do you judge your brother or sister? Or you*
> *as well, why do you regard your brother or sister with contempt?*
> *For we will all appear before the judgment seat of God."*
> ~ Romans 14:10

Love is the foundation for stewarding dreams for others. The Father is watching. We are custom designed to partner with the Holy Spirit, and wherever He empowers, life and freedom is released.

How we say what we say really does matter. We can choose to communicate through presumption, shaming, and usurping. Or we can deliver a message with honor, deference, and love. At the heart of it, the goal is to encourage, speak life, and pray into what God is showing—knowing that He's always at work behind the scenes. As Paul said, *"Let all you do be done in love."* [54]

> The role of an individual with some sort of prophetic message is simply to *deliver a message.*

REFLECTIONS

1. Do you first ask God how a dream featuring someone else applies to you? Before assuming it's about others, do you reflect on your own role in the dream?

_____

_____

_____

2. Do you actively seek God's wisdom on how, when, and where to share the dream?

_____

_____

_____

3. How do you react when someone doesn't act on a dream you've shared? Do you find it difficult to release the outcome to God?

_____

_____

_____

4. When you pray for someone based on a dream, do you focus on their destiny rather than their faults?

_____

_____

_____

5. Are you trusting God with the timing and outcome after sharing a dream? How can you leave the results in God's hands?

_____

_____

_____

C h a p t e r 1 2

RECEIVING A DREAM
FROM OTHERS

Earlier this year, I was talking with the Lord about whether Dave and I were on the same page. Specifically, if Dave was receiving the wisdom and direction he needed during these tumultuous times on the earth. I had just heard a message about a dream in which the current plans of God's Kingdom were symbolized by a hidden "nuclear" test site. A few days later, Dave's sister called to tell me she had the following dream.

Dream:

> *"I had a dream that you, your mom, and my mom were walking outside together. Kathy was to my left. My mom and Kathy's mom were to my right. Kathy said to me quietly that Dave was working on something "nuclear," but she couldn't talk about it. Then she said, 'Dave and I are solid,' with a very happy look on her face."*

When I heard this dream, I felt a wave of joy and relief. God answered my concerns by releasing intel *through someone else's dream*. This dream held a clear message, using the word "nuclear" to reassure me that we were on the right track and that Dave was perfectly positioned at the heart of what God was doing.

As your dream community grows, whether within your family, friend group, or church, it's likely that someone will have a dream involving you and will want to share it with you. Which can be exciting. Or awkward. Or vulnerable. Or incredibly encouraging.

We Are Responsible For What We Do With The Dream

The first principle to anchor into when given a dream (or any message someone believes is from God) is that *we* are responsible for what we do with it. God always holds *us* responsible for *our* behavior. He charges us to walk by the Spirit, so we won't act according to the flesh.

> *"But I say, walk by the Spirit,*
> *and you will not carry out the desire of the flesh."*
> ~ Galatians 5:16

In other words, we are to evaluate everything that comes our way through the discernment and empowerment of the Holy Spirit, and in light of the Scriptures.

I've heard repeated stories of individuals who were given a prophetic message of some kind, whether a word or a dream, and took it as God's absolute direction only later to endure disastrous results. These individuals subsequently rejected anything that could be considered a *rhema* message from God. While painful to hear, there's a key element missing in these cases - *taking personal responsibility for their own actions*.

Many voices in the Body of Christ decry all things dreams, visions, or prophetic messages because people have been hurt in the process.

They've determined that it's too risky, too messy, and they don't want to take any chances. They set aside the scriptural mandate,

"Do not despise prophecies, but test everything;
hold fast to what is good."
~ 1 Thessalonians 5:20, 21

When encountering these objections, I've often shared my experience in that I've been far more injured by teachers mishandling or weaponizing the written word of God than through any prophetic words given to me.

The Bereans stand as a timeless example of the ideal approach—eager to learn, yet careful to measure everything against Scripture. The Lord commends those who don't quickly accept any message but instead, they measure it — whether it's a teaching or prophecy — against the whole of Scripture and with the confirmation of the Holy Spirit.

"Now the Berean Jews were of more noble character than those in
Thessalonica, for they received the message with great eagerness and
examined the Scriptures every day to see if what Paul said was true."
~ Acts 17:11

Value What God Values And Stay In Peace

If the Lord took the trouble to entrust someone with a dream for us, or so they believe, once again, we are to value what God values. Like the parable of the talents, the Master gave his servants a deposit. He expected them to invest what he entrusted to them.

With this in mind, if someone tells you a dream that they believe is for you, consciously communicate with the Holy Spirit and listen with an open heart. Keep in mind that *you answer to God, not to this individual.* Also, keep in mind that when someone shares a dream they believe has a message for us, it can feel vulnerable for both the dreamer and the recipient. So, stay in peace. Remember that the Lord is your shield, He is for you; reject fear.[55]

Respond in Love While Honoring Your Boundaries.

Once they share the dream, it's up to you how to move forward with it. If you want to discuss it further with them, that's great. You can ask them how they felt about it or if they have revelation on it. *But you are not obligated to.* We are not indebted to *anyone* for sharing whatever kind of prophetic message. They are just the *messenger and not the counselor.* A friendly "Thanks for sharing" is perfectly appropriate.

> Keep in mind that *you answer to God, not to this individual.*

Regardless of who it is or how insistent they are, we answer to God, not to them.

Maybe the dream they shared doesn't resonate with you. Even so, respond lovingly and respectfully. Perhaps, "I'll take a look at that," or "Hmm. That's interesting." Resist any pressure to follow up with them. That's not how this works. If it does resonate, record it and discuss it with the Lord. Keep reviewing it and praying over it.

Our responses to one another when discussing dreams can make or break the health of a dream community. On the one hand, if we are overly sensitive and become offended when a friend shares a dream they believe is for us, we'll greatly hamper future dialogue. On the other hand, if we feel obligated to assure them or tell them how this might apply to our lives, we set an atmosphere where others expect vulnerability or to be included in our process if they approach us with a dream.

Steward Dreams or Words that are From the Lord

If you discern that the dream or word is indeed from the Lord, steward it the same way you would if it were your own dream. Record it. Pray over it asking God to give even more revelation. If the message contains a promise, steward that promise by engaging your will and agreeing with it. Declare the promise out loud. Write it out and keep it where you'll see it often. Remember, what we focus on we empower.

If the message contains a correction, repent first to the Lord, confess it to a trusted individual,[56] and then make amends to anyone you may have injured in some way. If the thought of intentionally approaching someone to admit you were wrong, to seek forgiveness, and to make things right feels overwhelming, take heart—I want to offer you some encouragement. Not only are we instructed to do this in scripture and receive the approval of the Lord when doing so, it is rare that we are met with disdain or anger. Scripture commands us to take this step, and the Lord delights in our obedience.[57] And more often than we expect, others respond with mercy, not anger. Amazingly, when we humble ourselves and admit our wrongs, it can actually deepen trust and foster goodwill in the relationship.

In short, when someone shares a dream they believe is meant for you, approach it with an open heart and a prayerful attitude. It's crucial to test everything and take responsibility for how you respond. Ask clarifying questions to gain a clearer understanding of the dream, but don't feel obligated to respond right away. Whether or not it resonates, honor the process and keep your focus on what God is saying to you. Our experience is that a community rooted in healthy dialogue and respect will produce profound and lasting fruit. (More on dream community protocol in Chapter 18.)

REFLECTIONS

1. Have you had someone share a dream they believe is for you? How did you respond?

_____

_____

_____

2. When receiving a prophetic message, what steps can you take to ensure you evaluate it through the lens of the Holy Spirit?

_____

_____

_____

3. How can you practice honoring dreams and prophetic words while maintaining personal responsibility in how you respond to them?

_____

_____

_____

4. How can you create an atmosphere of peace and respect when discussing dreams with others in your dream community?

_____

_____

_____

5. What can you do to steward a dream from someone else that feels like it's from God?

_____

_____

_____

Chapter 13

CHILDREN AND DREAMS

Dream:

> *"The dream was about a play in the middle of nowhere. They split us into groups, and they made us choose an actor, but it wasn't acting, it was like real life where you would actually die. When it was our group's turn, they chose me to be the actor. Then they brought out this live Tupperware dog that was biting me and trying to kill me. I was fighting the dog because I didn't want to die, and I won."*

The young boy who had this dream learned several things through processing it. The attacking dog represented fake/plastic friends who, for whatever reason, were trying to take him out through slander. The dreamer learned to "not be afraid, because the Lord is fighting with me to fight the evil dog."

One of the greatest privileges in life is helping to set up future generations for deeper intimacy with God, a heightened fear of the Lord, greater freedom, and increased power in establishing righteousness on the earth.

Since dreams and encounters with the Lord are pivotal to our spiritual growth, it's essential to prepare the next generation to understand and interpret these experiences. This also highlights the importance of training those who mentor and influence the young ones.

"Your children do not have to live with or tolerate nightmares. It is not the norm."

Trisha, my wonderful friend and mother of four dynamic kids, passionately shared this when I recently reached out to her to collaborate regarding children and dreams. She went on to say, *"We need to do our job as parents to protect them. They're tormented, and we dismiss it. They're scared to go to bed, so we give them melatonin, a blankie, cuddle them and say bedtime prayers."*

In our culture today, many parents are overlooking the importance and impact of their children's dreams. Often, dreams are dismissed as mere products of an active imagination rather than being recognized as potentially containing valuable messages. Many have no paradigm in which dreams matter. Instead of processing their kids' nightmares and then leveraging them to shut the enemy down and release them to thrive, many parents use the only tools they know - offering comfort and a quick prayer. The reality is that we possess authority over evil and are privy to the counsel of Almighty God. So do our children. This chapter is to encourage you to get trained up to turn around and do just that with the children in your life.

"'In the last days, God says,
I will pour out my Spirit on all people.
Your sons and daughters will prophesy,
your young men will see visions,
your old men will dream dreams.
Even on my servants, both men and women,
I will pour out my Spirit in those days,
and they will prophesy.
~ Acts 2:17, 18

I am convinced this next generation is going to put Acts 2:17-18 on display like no other generation before them. And the generations to follow will only increase after them. Not only will they walk in the fear of the Lord, fully captivated by His Presence, but the Holy Spirit will pour out revelation, wonders, and power through them in ways the world has never witnessed. They will carry a deep passion for unity and a relentless pursuit of Truth. They will lead many of us into a deeper understanding of God's ways, and through their influence, our love for the Lord will grow exponentially. Countless prodigals will return, stepping into their Kingdom assignments, as they experience the overwhelming reality of Jesus' love and the transformative power of the Holy Spirit within them!

It's already happening.

I've watched this reality play out in our home group over the past seven years. Many of us initially connected through the dream workshops I was teaching. This group came together out of a deep hunger to understand and faithfully steward the ways of the Holy Spirit within a community. They are biblically grounded and mature brothers and sisters who are passionate about joining with the Holy Spirit and operating in all the gifts and tools we were created to wield as the Ekklesia.

Among these Jesus-loving warriors are singles and families of all ages, from newborns to college students, with nieces and nephews, children and grandchildren represented across the generations. The parents are serious about not only saturating their families in the Scriptures but also teaching their kids *and* partnering with them to understand and operate in prophetic skills. They consistently practice recognizing the Lord's Presence, discerning the voice of the Holy Spirit, speaking prophetic words over others, declaring God's will, and exercising authority over enemy intrusions. Alongside this, they deeply value, interpret, and steward dreams.

We are not unique. I am thrilled to see this model exploding within the church today.

Trisha and her husband Joel are a beautiful example of growing in this as a family. I met them at a time when they were combatting an evil presence in their home. A friend and I were invited to their home to pray with them, do some spiritual house cleaning, and ask the Lord for wisdom. As a result of this "problem," the Lord propelled their family into a journey of getting trained up in spiritual weapons and operating in their spiritual gifts. The battle over that issue wasn't resolved in a day, but they simply couldn't deny the spiritual realities in their home any longer.

Speaking of problems not going away in a day, have you ever noticed that a roadblock in resolving an issue is just what the Lord leverages to catapult us into a new dimension of His Kingdom? This means that when we find ourselves stuck, we can expect a coming breakthrough and a deeper level of intimacy with the Lord, along with a greater understanding of His ways. God is a master at working all things to His and our advantage.

Back to our friends on their journey. During this season, their kids were receiving vivid dreams, and the dreams were coming with such frequency. The parents took these dreams seriously, considering them vital to the welfare of the whole family.

They began recording their dreams, and the entire family joined together to partner with the Holy Spirit, seeking to understand their meanings and how to apply them. Each of the kids would contribute "connecting pieces" that gave insight into what they were experiencing in the home. The *children* were the vehicle God was using to bring them into this realm of communication from Heaven.

"The Lord knew I would question myself. We just couldn't deny that the Lord was speaking in dreams. It unified us. It helped alleviate our skepticism and unbelief. The Lord woke us up!"

I was so impressed watching them learn *with* their children as they took on this challenge in unfamiliar and often intimidating territory. I once asked Trisha how she knew to include the kids and respect their perspective. I laughed at her response,

"I was desperate! For me, it was all hands-on deck!" she said without hesitation. She went on to explain, *"We were all walking in the process of learning in the journey. We weren't afraid of letting our kids see that 'we don't know.' We would say things like, 'Here's where I am on that' or 'Let's seek the Lord' or 'We don't know, let's ask.' It gave permission to learn for the kids. It opened us up as a family so that everyone felt like they had a part. No one had all the answers."*

Incredible. I believe their story is a prototype for how kids and dreams were meant to operate in the Body of Christ. This family was just one of many in our circle that I watched in wonder as they caught the wind of recognizing and responding to the Holy Spirit, especially as He spoke to their children through various supernatural means.

> Dreams are one of the few places where a child is completely on their own.

When it comes to dreams, supporting children is especially important. Have you ever thought about how dreams are one of the few places where a child is completely on their own? They can easily feel isolated in the dream realm. That's one reason why it's essential to encourage them, walk alongside them, empower them, and equip them.

Listening to children's dreams is one of my absolute favorite things. Their perspectives are not bound by the same limitations adults often develop. They haven't yet been conditioned to dismiss fantastical images or experiences. For a child, flying feels completely natural, and possessing superhero strength seems perfectly reasonable.

And when you think about it, why not?! We are, after all, designed to operate in the supernatural realm. I love the way they describe what they've experienced. Typically, they don't feel embarrassed telling their dreams, which is refreshing.

As adults, we often categorize dream experiences as "crazy," "nonsensical," or "weird." But a quick read through Ezekiel or Revelation can help normalize the strange and mysterious things we encounter in dreams. We have to admit that God's creativity in the unseen realm is pretty out of the box for us.

For many, engaging children in the conversation of the supernatural realm is a new and uncomfortable concept. It certainly was for me. I'll admit, I still feel awkward sometimes. But Jesus Himself encourages us to humble ourselves and embrace children and their childlike ways.

> *"Truly I tell you, unless you change and become like little children, you will never enter the kingdom of heaven. Therefore, whoever takes the lowly position of this child is the greatest in the kingdom of heaven."*
> ~ Matthew 18:2-4

If we dismiss, minimize, or explain away the dreams and perceptions of children, the consequences can be significant. Not only will we likely diminish their sense of worth, but we'll also likely miss the Father's communication—often in the form of warnings—and allow the enemy to stay hidden, operating freely within the home.

Value their journey and record their insights, dreams and experiences.

On the other hand, a huge advantage to valuing our children's spiritual perception is that the unseen realm will become more visible to us.[58] Just like the greater Body of Christ, we need all the parts working together to function as a whole.[59]

Making Dreams and Interpretation Part of the Family Conversation

As you navigate this journey, here are some strategies we've found to be particularly effective in helping children with their dreams:

- Make space for their input.
- Share dreams around the table.

- Approach a child the same as an adult, only with language they understand.
- Honor children as equal in receiving revelation from Holy Spirit. Eli demonstrated this with young Samuel.[60]
- Model the dream interpretation process in your own life.
- Include them in the interpretation process.
- When they tell a dream, ask lots of clarifying questions.
- Suggest they draw the dream.
- Have them voice record and then later write it for them in a journal (especially the young ones).
- Help them discern the source of the dream and the focus of the dream. (Remember, if they take themselves out of the dream, does the dream fall apart?)
- Help them ask "why this and not that?" with elements in their dream.
- Together, ask the Lord what the dream means.
- Wait to open up dream symbols until you've asked the Lord. Look at resources when you get stuck.
- Train them to discern the voice of the Lord.
- If you feel you struggle in discerning the voice of the Lord, ask the Holy Spirit to show you examples in His word. Ask Him to help you, and to find other believers more experienced in this.

Bottom line, value their journey and record their insights, dreams and experiences. I promise, you will build a rich record of the Lord's guidance, reassurance, and communication within your family. I encourage you to look around for like-minded believers to walk this out. Search for a mentor who is further down the road.

Why are my kids having nightmares?

One of the most helpless feelings we can experience as parents or grandparents is when a child experiences a nightmare, especially when they endure repeated ones. Unfortunately, there has been a normalization of kids getting nightmares, night terrors and seeing spiritual manifestations. We hear,

"It's only a season."
"They're hallucinating."
"It's a phase."
"They'll outgrow it."

Although Dave and I had no formal training in dream interpretation and very little understanding of authority in spiritual warfare, we took our boys' nightmares seriously when they were young. With our limited knowledge at the time, we made it a priority to explore why they were being tormented. We didn't know much, but we understood enough to recognize that nightmares don't happen without a reason.

Did they see something in their room? (Kids often do see the spirit realm while many of us have been conditioned out of that ability.) We'd ask them what they saw or what their dream was and then, the best we knew how, we'd pray targeted prayers of authority based on that information.

We would then ask ourselves—and the Lord—what might have been allowed into our home that could be tormenting them. Or what might they have encountered during the day that left them vulnerable to the enemy's terror? Although we walked it out imperfectly, this perspective opened a safe space for our young kids to share difficult or traumatic events.

The dream realm is sacred ground. And there is a battle over who or what gets to occupy that space. Just look again at the world-changing revelations or messages that were given in dreams. It is a battlefield, and the enemy targets children. He targets their supernatural "receivers." He wants to dull their senses through trauma, fear, confusion, and isolation.

Why is that? Because dreams are a gift from God and He loves to speak to children, to all of us, in dreams. The enemy is terrified of our communion with Almighty God. That communion is the seedbed of his defeat. He is desperate and wants to steal their sleep and push them to be afraid to dream. It's one of his ruthless schemes. Unfortunately, many of us have been unaware of his schemes, normalizing them with natural physiological explanations.

> "...so that no advantage would be taken of us by satan,
> for we are not ignorant of his schemes."
> ~ 2 Corinthians 2:11

When it comes to kids and nightmares, there *is* a cause and effect.

I understand how overwhelming the terror children experience in nightmares and dark encounters can feel for us as parents, grandparents, and friends. I've certainly felt that fear and the weight of being overwhelmed myself. The enemy wants us to believe we're powerless in these situations. But we are not helpless! We are not at the mercy of scare tactics. We already have the victory through Jesus' death and resurrection. We have tools to not only defeat these evil intrusions, but we also have tools to empower children to grow more in love with Jesus and to do great damage to the kingdom of darkness.

The dream realm is sacred ground. And there is a battle over who or what gets to occupy that space.

If nightmares are becoming a frequent occurrence for a child, ask the Lord, "Why is this happening?" Pray for the Holy Spirit to open your eyes to any influences in the home that might be allowing the enemy to cause distress. Ask Him to reveal any situations or experiences that could be negatively impacting your child and be ready to receive whatever He uncovers. It could be something as simple as a TV show they're watching or a video game they've been playing. Or it could be something more serious, like feeling embarrassed at school or even experiencing abuse.

The choices of adults or older siblings can also invite unwanted enemy interference. Anxiety in the home—whether it's over financial struggles or a friend or relative going through a difficult time—can stir up fear and nightmares. Engaging with things like inappropriate videos, shows, or internet searches can create an entry point for dark spiritual influences. Items related to the occult in the home – tarot cards, a Ouija board, horoscopes, crystals, artifacts or artwork dedicated to other gods – are all "legal" grounds for the enemy to intrude and harass.[61]

When persistent nightmares occur, ask the Lord to help your child verbalize what's happening in their life.

When persistent nightmares occur, ask the Lord to help your child verbalize what's happening in their life. He will guide them. Create a safe space where they feel comfortable sharing. Regardless of the source of the nightmares, God is faithful and will provide wisdom.[62] He has already equipped us with the weapons and authority we need.

Be Lovers of Truth

It takes courage to seek understanding behind the cause of children's nightmares. But the Spirit of Jesus in us *is courageous*. God never reveals things to embarrass, shame, or punish us. He reveals things to give us the opportunity to repent, or to receive healing and restoration through His overcoming power. He brings things to the surface so that we can deal with them, liberating us to live more fully in His love, power, and freedom.

"Surely You desire truth in the inmost being;
You teach me wisdom in the inmost place."
~ Psalm 51:6 BSB

Whether trying to help a child enduring nightmares or simply in our own walk with God, we must be *lovers of truth* first and foremost. We've discussed the "fear of being deceived." From what I understand so far, we are much more likely to be deceived about *our own lives* and circumstances than we are about theology.

Ask the Lord for clarity on His truth in your current situation. He is faithful. If we seek, we *will* find - it's a promise. Remember, regardless of how painful the answer turns out to be, when God reveals something, that means His power is present to heal and overcome. He reveals to heal.

We must come to terms with the fact that *truth is not the enemy*. It's the very thing that sets us free and leads us to the heart of God. The enemy of our souls is trying to deceive us and instill false fear to replace the fear of the Lord. I remember hearing an illustration that vividly put this into perspective:

> *Late one night, a woman left a gas station after paying inside the store. As soon as she pulled onto the street, she noticed a man following her in his car. Her heart raced as she pressed the gas pedal, hoping to shake him, but he stayed right on her tail. Panic set in. Desperate, she quickly mapped the nearest police station and sped toward it, the man still in hot pursuit.*
>
> *She screeched into the parking lot, tires burning as she slammed to a stop. Frantically, she jumped out of her car, only to see the man leap from his vehicle and race toward her. Heart pounding, she sprinted toward the police station, shouting for help. But just as she neared the door, the man dashed right past her, flinging open the back door of her car.*
>
> *To her shock, he revealed a hidden attacker, lying in wait. The truth hit her with a sickening wave: the man she thought was threatening her was actually her savior, and the real danger had been silently lurking in the shadows all along.*

We must constantly remind ourselves that our battle is not against flesh and blood, but against unseen principalities, powers, and rulers of darkness.[63] The ones in the shadows. We are instructed to come against the "wiles of the devil" - the enemy's evil schemes - by putting on the full armor of God, standing, praying in the Spirit on all occasions with all kinds of prayers and requests, and remaining alert.[64]

> We must be *lovers of truth* first and foremost.

I encourage you to pause right now and ask God to reveal what is currently hidden. Be honest about any fear you might have about the potential consequences of facing the truths He may show you. He understands our fears and weaknesses.

> *"Just as a father has compassion on his children, so the Lord has compassion on those who fear Him. For He Himself knows our frame; He is mindful that we are but dust."*
> ~ Psalm 103:13-14

Ask Him to forgive you for any fear and to cleanse you from all unrighteousness. Tell Him you are willing to receive whatever He reveals to you.

Practical Steps for Addressing Nightmares

With all of this in mind, here are some practical tools and helpful strategies for addressing children's nightmares:

- Before they share their nightmare, bind shame and fear. "In the name of Jesus, I bind shame and fear."
- Agree with them that it is scary, but fear is not from the Lord.
- Tell fear to go in Jesus' name. Command, "No spirit but the Holy Spirit!"
- Give focused attention on them as you have them tell the dream.
- Bless them in the name of Jesus.

- Ask the Lord to wash them clean and remove the trauma of experiencing a nightmare.
- Flip the dream - declare the Lord's plan using the dream as a springboard. Help them to flip the dream and to declare with their mouth.
- Take authority over any demonic presence. "In Jesus name, I bind you and send you to Jesus for judgment." Teach them their authority.
- Ask God for justice and, according to Scripture, demand the enemy repay.[65]
- Pray for God to erase the defiling images in the dream.

Equipping Children to Navigate Nightmares

- Have them say, "Fear is a liar" – say it out loud. Say it louder.
- Turn toward the intruder or fear and speak to it, telling it to go.
- Say the name of Jesus. "Jesus, Jesus, Jesus."
- Teach them that God is their armor. He is their shield.
- Affirm that God is the Lord of Hosts – Commander of angel armies. Teach them God is the ultimate authority.
- Equip them to say in a dream, "Fear is a liar!"
- Equip them to call on Jesus in a dream.
- Together, memorize key Scriptures that declare our authority.

> Courage, faith, and authority are built up in children and in us as we wrestle with these attacks and win.

Courage, faith, and authority are built up in children and in us as we wrestle with these attacks and win. Our friends were delighted to discover that once the children became confident in their authority and the enemy's tactics, they were successfully dealing with nightmares on their own. They were not even coming to wake their parents up at night.

Dreams with kids are an adventure *and* a challenge! It can be awkward, vulnerable, exposing, uncomfortable. But the rewards are invaluable. Embracing and exploring dreams with your kids opens up a whole new realm of discovering how God has uniquely gifted each family member. Each one contributes with different supernatural abilities, given by the Holy Spirit for the benefit of the others.

Set aside any worry about getting it right all the time. Making mistakes along the way is part of the process. And the process *is* the purpose – it's not the end goal.

REFLECTIONS

1. What are some common misconceptions about nightmares in children, and how can you help reframe them from a biblical perspective?

    _____

    _____

    _____

2. Did you struggle with nightmares as a kid? How were they handled in your home?

    _____

    _____

    _____

3. How can you create a family culture where spiritual dreams and experiences are normalized, honored, and discussed openly?

    _____

    _____

    _____

4. Are any objects in your home coming to mind that may need to be removed?

_____

_____

_____

5. What specific prayers or declarations can be helpful when dealing with children's nightmares, and how can they be integrated into family life regularly? Do you feel like you need more help in knowing how to do this?

_____

_____

_____

Chapter 14

HELPING OTHERS
WITH DREAMS

Now, we're stepping into the exciting realm of helping *others* understand their dreams. This is where dream interpretation gets FUN! Well, sort of fun. Honestly, it can be a little nerve-wracking.

Wearing our metaphorical swim-goggles and armed with our biblical dream symbols, numbers, and colors, we take a deep breath and dive in with the Holy Spirit. Suddenly things aren't as clear as we'd hoped they'd be. Unexpected challenges are hiding beneath the surface. Symbols and scenarios not mentioned in the Bible or in our books confront us. We have trouble visualizing someone else's dream, much less articulating its possible meaning. We start to feel flustered. People can get angry or defensive.

Like I said, this is where it gets fun!

Dream:

> *I dreamt that I was helping my friend clean out her room at the end of the school year. As we were taking things to her car, I realized that I had stolen some stuff from the school. I*

didn't seem to feel concerned about having stolen something and reasoned that I probably didn't need to tell anyone about it. We left to get food. As we were walking toward my car, I realized that there were two dead bodies in my trunk. I knew I had killed them. Again, I wasn't overly concerned with that either. I was just casually thinking that I didn't need to tell anybody about either the stolen items or the dead bodies, and it would all work out.

This dream was current day, and the coloring was bright. But all the people in the dream were kind of exaggerated and puffy and bouncy. Almost like in an animated cartoon.

One evening, my sister, Karen, called me with this dream. We had both attended John Paul Jackson's dream courses together and had been processing each other's dreams for years, so we were very comfortable in that space. I respect her deeply, and at first, I was hesitant to interpret the dream as something negative in her life, especially since she was clearly the focal point of the dream. I told her I really wanted to file it under the "false dream" category, but I hadn't received confirmation from the Holy Spirit. I thought to myself, "Surely, the Lord didn't intend to correct her through this!"

Remember that one of the key principles is "stay true to the dream"? I was really struggling to apply that here.

I asked her to give me a few minutes to change into my PJ's and that I'd pray on it. During that time, I mused with the Lord about the elements of the dream – murder, stealing, and exaggerated puffy, bouncy people. I mentally searched through Scriptures for these concepts. All at once, it clicked.

I called her back, and our conversation went something like this: *"Hey, I was thinking about the murders and how Jesus said that if we hate another person, it's like murder.*[66] *Are you by any chance holding on to any unforgiveness?"*

Her immediate reply was, *"Yep, I know exactly what that's about."*

Encouraged that we were on the right track, I went on to say that I believed stealing items in the dream was an equivalent of coveting. These two unaddressed issues, unforgiveness and coveting, were distorting her perception of the people around her.

I want you to know that Karen embodies a key trait we talked about in the chapter on intrinsic dreams. She is fully committed to obeying whatever God shows her and keeps her heart open to whatever He might reveal. True to form, that night she dedicated a concentrated time with the Lord repenting of unforgiveness. She asked God for clarity on what she had been coveting and quickly repented.

When someone comes to you with a dream – and I hope they do – how exactly do you best partner with them to find the interpretation? Although I've illustrated this process throughout the book, I'll outline it more thoroughly in this chapter.

Relax, It's Not About You

Believe me, it is tempting to put pressure on ourselves when helping someone else with dreams. But seriously, it is not about us.

A few years back, I was invited to be a guest on a YouTube podcast, The Remnant Radio, focusing on theology, church history, and the gifts of the Spirit.[67] My dear friend, Suzanna, introduced me to one of the hosts, Michael Miller, and over a cup of coffee, he asked if I'd be willing to come on the show to talk about biblical dream interpretation. He put me at ease right away, and because I'm always excited to talk about dreams, I happily agreed, saying, "Sure, I'd love to!"

When I got home after our meeting, I thought it would be a good idea to research some of the interviews with previous guests. You know, just get a feel for their show. Colossal mistake. World-renowned theologians, international speakers, and celebrated authors.

My internal alarm bells went off, and I started panicking. Thoughts raced through my mind, like, "These people are way out of my league.

I can't go on this show. Besides, their listeners are into deep theological topics – they're not going to want to hear about dream interpretation. I have to cancel. Immediately!"

I grabbed my phone to text Suzanna, the instigator behind this outrageous idea, ready to back out and say I couldn't do this after all. Just before I hit "send," a text from her dinged through.

"Hey, they just announced live on the show that you're going to be a guest!"

I was stuck. No backing out now, much to my dismay.

Fortunately, the date for the interview was still a few months away. A lot could happen in a few months, I reasoned. And it did. The Lord got to work on *me*. Over the next few weeks, He helped me realize that I was focused on *myself* rather than on the opportunity He had offered me. (I know that seems obvious as you read this story - it's certainly obvious to me in hindsight - but when you're in the middle of all of the emotions, it's rarely that clear.) I began to get excited about the show as I came into alignment with His heart. My fears dissipated, and I eventually reached a state of unshakeable peace.

Or so I thought.

Two days prior to the broadcast, Michael called me to finalize details about the interview. Just before hanging up, he added, *"Oh hey, you don't mind doing live dream interpretation on the show, do you?"* Gulp. Fresh wave of panic.

The next day I called a friend to ask for prayer. She listened patiently as I described the latest request and my newfound anxiety. When I finished, there was a pregnant pause on the other end of line. She thoughtfully responded, *"Hmm. Well, I guess it's still about you then, isn't it?"*

Wise, discerning, and direct—everyone needs friends like this. She prayed with me, helping me break agreement with fear and pride, and together, we put the whole situation in God's hands.

As it turned out, I thoroughly enjoyed the podcast on dreams and soon Dave and I developed a cherished friendship with Michael and his family. The Holy Spirit gave rich insight during the live dream interpretation. In fact, months later, the podcast team received an incredible testimony from a listener who shared how the recounting of one of the live dreams created a supernatural atmosphere in their home, leading to the miraculous healing of their young son's severe epilepsy.

God is up to *much more* than we can imagine. Relax, it's not about you.

Tell the Whole Dream And Nothing but the Dream

When someone asks for help with a dream, encourage them to tell you the entire dream. Recommend that they leave any context or commentary out. For the dreamer, this can be a challenge for a couple of reasons. Telling a dream can feel vulnerable and it's tempting for them to want to fill in the gaps as they tell the dream. Also, they often want to "help" you along by describing their current circumstances or giving context to the people in the dream.

The problem with this is that adding or subtracting or emphasizing one aspect over another can detract from the actual message. We are trying to stay true to the dream itself.

Maintain an Open Dialogue with the Holy Spirit (Maintain Communication)

Engaging your spirit is crucial when listening to a dream. I have found this to be a learned skill in my life. Back in the day at the biblical dream interpretation conferences I attended, we would inevitably break into small groups to practice. Operating in these ways was entirely foreign territory for me, and all my focus would go to dream elements and what they could mean. Whenever someone would mention the Holy Spirit, I'd inwardly snap out of my back-in-college intellectual approach and think, "Oh right. The Holy Spirit. I should probably be consulting with Him."

As they launch into the dream, begin to pray - this is a partnership between you and the Lord.

"When the Spirit of truth comes, he will guide you into all truth."
~ John 16:13

It's not complicated – a simple "help!" is enough to shift our awareness and invite the Spirit's supernatural influence. Ask the Lord to help you discern His communication. Pay attention to thoughts, images, or feelings as you are listening.

Listen Attentively While Visualizing the Dream in Your Spirit

Be fully present while listening to the dream, noting details and visualizing it in your spirit. Remember, spiritual dreams are real encounters in the spirit realm.

> Spiritual dreams are real encounters in the spirit realm.

I had an unexpected experience that perfectly illustrates visualizing a dream with your spirit. One evening at a seminar, early in my dream-teaching journey, I finished presenting, and the participants began sharing their dreams. A newfound friend was partway through telling a dream when I interrupted her, *"Have you told me this dream?"* She answered that she hadn't. I went on to say, *"I know this dream. I can see it, and I know what happens next and how it ends!"*

In my spirit, I could literally see the dream as if I'd dreamed it myself. She finished sharing the dream, and it confirmed what the Holy Spirit had already shown me. In this case, the dream's interpretation aligned seamlessly with a calling she had been sensing from the Lord. The fact that the Lord revealed the dream to me before she even finished telling it served as a confirmation of the direction in which the Lord was taking her.

Ask Clarifying Questions

For most of us, describing dreams is a learned skill. If the dreamer isn't accustomed to the dream interpretation process, they often leave out details and context. Or they don't notice some aspects of the dream until they are prompted with helpful questions. For example, they might not have mentioned that it happened at night, or that they were just observing the whole time, or that the house on fire wasn't actually being consumed, or that they felt no fear despite the intense, heart-pounding circumstances.

Also, because dreams take place in a realm unbound by space, time, and gravity, questions are often needed to make sense of what the dreamer experienced.

Once, a dreamer was relating a dream in which they were driving on an overpass that felt like a roller coaster. The road abruptly ended, and the car went over the edge. End of dream.

It took a few questions to uncover that the car didn't *fall* but actually started *flying*, and the dreamer felt a sense of euphoria.

Here are a few questions I've found helpful:

- Was the dream full-color, muted, or black and white?
- How did you feel in the dream?
- What does that person represent to you?
- Is the dream current day?
- What stood out to you in this dream?
- Have you had similar dreams before?

Repeat the Dream Back to the Dreamer

Once you've clarified the entire dream, try repeating it back from start to finish. I know this can feel a bit intimidating, especially in a group setting, but it's a great way to test if you're truly following the dream's flow. It definitely gets easier with practice.

Repeating the dream is remarkably effective in helping someone with their dream. To begin with, it communicates value to the dreamer. When you repeat their dream back to them, it shows that you've truly heard them. It lets them know you're invested in both them and their dream, making sure you understand it accurately. This alone is a huge gift—it's a powerful way to demonstrate the Father's love, as you're genuinely listening with the intent to understand.

Hearing their dream retold, often for the first time, can also unlock revelation within the dreamer. They might pick up on word plays, feel emotions, or see elements they hadn't before. This phase of the process also affords the dreamer the opportunity to correct where we may have misunderstood them or to add additional information. It's amazing how often the dreamer will say, "Oh wait, I forgot about this part. There was also..."

Use Encouraging Language

Once you have a full picture of their dream, it's time to move on to discussing the interpretation. I frequently begin by asking the dreamer what *they* think the dream means. This not only honors them in the process but also reinforces their ownership of the dream for both of us.

When you suggest an interpretation, be sure to communicate in positive, edifying language. Again, our heart posture and *how* we say *what* we say is almost as important as the accuracy of the interpretation. Remember Paul's whole noisy gong and clanging symbol analogy?

"If I speak with the tongues of men and of angels but have not love,
I have become a noisy gong or a clanging cymbal. If I have the gift of
prophecy and know all mysteries and all knowledge, and if I have all
faith so as to remove mountains but have not love, I am nothing."
~ 1 Corinthians 13:1, 2

Supposing the dreamer dreamt that their teeth are loose, and a few are missing. The interpretation could suggest that they are struggling to gain wisdom or understanding at the moment. (Teeth help us "chew on and digest.") We could wince after hearing the dream and rip off the Band-Aid saying, *"Wow, I hate to say this, but it seems like this dream is pointing to the fact that you're missing something important and that you have a hard time grasping what God is trying to show you."*

A humorous bit of exaggeration, I know. And technically, that does convey the meaning. But where does that leave them? Shamed with no hope. God *always* communicates hope. So, keeping in mind that every dream is an invitation to connect with God, a better response might be...

"This is a great dream. It's an invitation from God to ask Him for greater understanding of what He's trying to reveal to you. Is there any area in your life where you feel you need more wisdom?"

Whether or Not to Tell Them the Interpretation?

Even at this stage, it's key to rely on the Holy Spirit's guidance. Sometimes, He may prompt you to simply respond with compassion or affirm their worth and purpose.

I recall attending a Streams Ministries dream interpretation conference during a live dream interpretation session led by one of their trained staff teachers. While one woman related her dream, he listened with an expression of deep compassion. After she finished sharing the dream, he paused and spoke with deep empathy. *"You've been through some very difficult times in your life, haven't you?"* She began to weep. Her dream was never interpreted publicly. Instead, he encouraged her, assuring her that God was healing her and affirming her beautiful destiny yet to come.

A few years ago, while interpreting dreams in a large group, a young man with a ministry position shared his dream. Some parts were clear, but I couldn't grasp the Lord's interpretation. I offered some insights on various elements of his dream but let him know I didn't have a full interpretation, and we moved on. Later that evening, back at home, I reflected on his dream with the Holy Spirit. The next morning, I woke up with full clarity and understood the dream completely. I instantly realized why I hadn't received revelation about it in the public setting. It was a "current condition" dream, revealing some immaturity in his life. The Holy Spirit was correcting him and calling him to a higher standard of living in the ways of God. I believe the Father didn't want to embarrass His son in front of the group. I wrote out the interpretation and sent it to the dreamer for him to consider and pray through.

This brings up another important aspect of integrity in dream interpretation: If you don't have the interpretation, be honest about it. Don't try to force an answer. Remember, it's not about you. Sometimes, God can work more through your honesty than through your dream interpretation skills.

A friend hosted a Level 2 seminar in her home, and her husband had significant reservations about the whole process. Towering at an impressive 6'7", he loomed at the back of the room in an imposing stance, his arms crossed over his chest throughout the evening. At one point, I had the attendees split into small groups to interpret a dream that had just been shared. Ten minutes later, each group reported what they felt the Lord had revealed to them about the dream. One of the interpretations really resonated with the dreamer, and we all felt a shared confirmation from the Lord.

> If you don't have the interpretation, be honest about it. Don't try to force an answer.

I then told the group that I didn't have revelation about this particular dream myself. I emphasized how valuable it is to work together in discerning God's messages through dreams. Much to my surprise, when the evening ended, my friend's husband approached me and said something to the effect of, *"You know, I've been on the fence about this whole dream thing. But when you admitted you didn't know the interpretation, I could tell you weren't trying to make this about yourself. I'm all in now."*

Ask for Feedback

When you suggest an interpretation, ask the dreamer, *"Does that resonate with you?"* Often, you'll see a "lightbulb" moment when the dreamer exclaims, "Yes, that makes perfect sense!" At times, tears will unexpectedly well up as the Lord tenderly touches a deep place in their heart, bringing encouragement for something that has troubled them or is especially meaningful to them. They might experience the wonder and delight of unraveling a divinely crafted puzzle. When a metaphor or clever wordplay is revealed, it often sparks joy and laughter. When a fear dream is understood, flipped, and turned back on the enemy with authority, the dreamer is not only relieved but empowered and equipped!

Sometimes, however, the interpretation we suggest just doesn't land, no matter how well it covers the elements of the dream. Even this is valuable because we're actively seeking, and in the process, we've identified what *doesn't fit.* There is no "formula" to biblically grounded dream interpretation. If we try to force pieces of the dream together without divine insight, we wind up with a lifeless Frankenstein interpretation that leaves the dreamer unsatisfied.

Keep praying and "reasoning through" the dream with them, coming from different angles as the Holy Spirit leads. Once again, our goal isn't to be seen as the "dream expert." The person standing in front of us is the object of our Heavenly Father's fierce love. We are *serving* them in trying to help them understand this mystical communication they have experienced. Of course, we *do* want to understand the dream, but "getting it right" isn't the whole goal. The interpretation is revealed for the benefit of the dreamer, not to draw attention to the interpreter.

"As for me, this mystery has been revealed to me, not because I have more wisdom than anyone living, but in order that the interpretation might be made known to the king, and that you may understand the thoughts of your mind."
~ Daniel 2:30

Whether you hit the nail on the head in helping someone with their dreams or it's a swing and a miss, you're still partnering with them and the Lord in the journey of understanding His voice and communication. In doing so, *you* are a pleasure to the heart of the Father. You are caring about what He values and for the ones He loves. At the very least, those you invest in will have walked through the biblical dream interpretation process, and you might just help them uncover a significant gift that God has hidden within their dream!

REFLECTIONS

1. What key principles from this chapter can help you stay focused on the dream rather than on your interpretation or pressure to "get it right"?

_____

_____

_____

2. Why is it important to ask the dreamer to share the dream without providing additional context or interpretation?

_____

_____

_____

3. What is the value of repeating the dream back to the dreamer, and how can it help both you and the dreamer gain clarity and insight?

_____

_____

_____

4. What does it mean to "stay true to the dream," and how can misinterpretation occur when this is not practiced?

_____

_____

_____

5. Why is it important to use positive, edifying language when suggesting interpretations to others? How can language impact the dreamer's understanding and emotional response?

_____

_____

_____

Chapter 15

TROUBLESHOOTING – ENCOUNTERS WHILE SLEEPING

"Since I was little, with my natural vision I have seen manifestations of different beings in my room. These freaked me out for years. But recently, I was asleep and when I woke up and opened my eyes in the night, I saw a man's face coming through a tunnel. The image was in black and white. I closed my eyes and then opened them again. The man was still there. I told him that in the name of Jesus Christ he needed to leave. I was not frightened either time I saw his face even though I knew he was not supposed to be there. This was an intrusion. He left. How I handled this encounter was progress for me!" ~ K. B.

Although this book is primarily about dreams, multiple other phenomena occur while sleeping or upon waking that inform us of the "unseen" realm. We also see these encounters or experiences throughout the Bible.

Visions

One of the most common supernatural experiences is visions. "In a vision, one sees into the spirit realm or has perception of supernatural things. The natural senses are allowed to experience the invisible realm of the spirit." [68] Visions can occur while awake no matter what time of day or night, as was the case with Cornelius.

> *"One day at about three in the afternoon he had a vision. He distinctly saw an angel of God, who came to him and said, 'Cornelius!'"*
> ~ Acts 10:3

Visions can also arise during the night while asleep.

> *"In the first year of King Belshazzar of Babylon, Daniel had a dream with visions in his mind as he was lying in his bed."*
> ~ Daniel 7:1

> *"Then God spoke to Israel in the visions of the night, and said, 'Jacob, Jacob!'"*
> ~ Genesis 46:2

> *"I, the LORD, reveal myself to them in visions, I speak to them in dreams."*
> ~ Numbers 12:6

Visions may be internal (those seen with the mind's eye) or manifest externally (also known as an "open heaven" experience or "open vision").

> *"But Stephen, full of the Holy Spirit, looked up to heaven and saw the glory of God, and Jesus standing at the right hand of God. 'Look,' he said, 'I see heaven open and the Son of Man standing at the right hand of God.'"*
> ~ Acts 7:55-56.

"And I, Daniel, alone saw the vision, for the men who
were with me did not see the vision; but a great terror fell
upon them, so that they fled to hide themselves."
~ Daniel 10:7

Trances

The term for trance in Greek is 'ekstasis.' "A displacement (of the mind), bewilderment, ecstasy, a trance."[69] In this visionary state, the body is overridden by supernatural forces and perceives what is not readily available to the conscious mind. Perhaps one of the most well-known is Peter's vision in a trance. This experience released an earth changing paradigm shift. With Peter's, shall we say *dynamic* personality, I've often wondered if the Holy Spirit forced him to sit still while He delivered the mold-breaking message that in the new covenant, all foods are clean.

"…while the meal was being prepared, he fell into a
trance. He saw heaven opened and something like a large
sheet being let down to earth by its four corners."
~ Acts 10:10, 11

Lucid Dreaming

A lucid dream is when the dreamer becomes aware that they are dreaming and gains control over their actions within the dream. Daniel is a biblical example of this type of dream.

"Daniel had a dream with visions in his mind as he was lying in his bed…
As for me, Daniel, my spirit was deeply distressed within me,
*and the visions in my mind terrified me. **I approached** one of*
*those who were standing by and **asked him to clarify all this**.*
So he let me know the interpretation of these things…"
~ Daniel 7:15-16 CSB

Because we retain control of our faculties in a lucid dream, it's crucial that our actions align with God's ways. If the dream has dark purposes, command the will of God be done. If you're being threatened in a lucid dream, resist the enemy. If, like Daniel, the dream is a mystery, ask God to clarify it within the dream.

> Because we retain control of our faculties in a lucid dream, it's crucial that our actions align with God's ways.

Lucid dreaming can be a powerful realm for creativity and inventions. Our family has a deep love of Handel's Messiah, and we attend a performance nearly every Christmas. Handel wrote "Messiah" after first hearing it in a dream. Einstein's theory of relativity came to him in a dream about cows. The chemist Dmitri Mendeleev, the author of the periodic table, had recognized a pattern in the elements. While dreaming, he saw the table of elements perfectly formed. He wrote it down as soon as he woke up.

The Lord longs to release inventions, works of art, medical breakthroughs, business strategies, plans for societal healing, educational initiatives, and so much more into the earth. What if *you* are on His mind to be entrusted with something like this in a dream?

See / Sense / Hear a "Presence"

Many have experienced a presence when waking from sleep. You may or may not see it – sometimes you simply feel it.

If the presence is positive, the response is, *"Speak Lord, Your servant is listening."* (1 Samuel 3:17). Even a good presence can be terrifying – just look at all of the encounters in Scripture where angels manifested and people freaked out. Hence the repeated phrase, *"Fear not,"* when they appear. Nevertheless, no matter how intimidating, the Lord created the angels as ministering spirits, sent to assist us in fulfilling our assignments here on earth.

*"Are not all angels ministering spirits sent to serve
those who will inherit salvation?"*
~ Hebrews 4:14

Visitations from the Third Heaven

Visitations from the Third Heaven to the earthly realm are recorded throughout scripture and continue to happen today. One type of a Third Heaven visitation is a physical or auditory manifestation of God Himself, referred to as the "Angel of the Lord," otherwise known as a theophany. Hagar encountered the Angel of the Lord when in the desert after being evicted by Sarah, in Genesis 16:7, 8. A while later, Abraham also encountered the Lord in the form of a man (Genesis 18).

Throughout Scripture, there are numerous accounts of angelic visitations. Angels were dispatched to Lot (Genesis 19:1), and the Angel Gabriel appeared to Zechariah (Luke 1). Events surrounding Jesus' birth are chock-full of angelic appearances. And lest we limit angelic visitations to the pages of Scripture alone, there are numerous accounts of angels continuing to deliver messages, offer protection, and provide supernatural assistance to people over the centuries and even in our time.

On the Mount of Transfiguration, Peter, James, and John witnessed Moses and Elijah engaging Jesus (Matthew 17).

Hearing an Audible Voice

Experiencing a supernatural audible voice, whether it be the Lord's voice or that of an angel, is something we see in Scripture and that continues to occur today.

Moses heard God's voice from the burning bush where He revealed His plan to lead the Israelites out of Egypt. Abraham also encountered God's voice on multiple occasions, such as when God called him to leave his homeland and go to a land that He would show him. Elijah heard God's voice in the still, small whisper after a mighty wind, earthquake, and fire had passed. Samuel, as a young boy in the temple, heard his name called by God, marking his first encounter with the Lord. And in a vision while in the temple, Isaiah heard the voice of God commissioning him as a prophet, setting him on the path of his divine calling.[70] On one occasion, I was awakened from sleep to see an angel who looked just like me and heard a loud audible voice deliver a message in surround sound. Because 99% of my supernatural encounters as a child were demonic, I assumed this was as well. I rebuked it in Jesus' name and, undisturbed, went back to sleep. The next morning, I prayed about the message I'd heard. Later when I related this experience to John Paul Jackson, I was horrified to hear that it was *my* angel with a message. He laughed and said not to worry – he had done the same thing on several occasions. I later read in Acts where the believers mistook Peter for his angel. I realized then that it's actually common for our angels to appear in our own likeness.[71]

If we do experience hearing an audible voice and recognize it as coming from the Kingdom of Heaven, we can respond like Samuel did:

> *"Speak, Lord, your servant is listening."*
> ~ 1 Samuel 3:10

Dèjá Vu

It's not uncommon to encounter a situation in the natural that reminds us of a dream, or it might evoke the same feelings we experienced in a dream. Often, we don't "recall" being in this situation or forget that we've experienced it in a dream. Many consider this to be the source of "déjà vu." Déjà vu is an experience that nearly everyone encounters at some point. It serves as one way of receiving divine insight, which is incredibly helpful. When you experience déjà vu, ask the Lord for understanding of what you're experiencing in that moment and what

He might be revealing through it. Ask the Holy Spirit to help you apply His wisdom in your circumstance.

Recurring Dreams

I'm often asked about the significance of experiencing multiple dreams with the same theme. I went through a season where I repeatedly dreamed that I was back in school. A friend shared a series of dreams with me, all centered around the same theme: trying to pack a suitcase but having way too much stuff to fit in. I just received a message from a seminar attendee who shared that he's been having a recurring dream about desperately needing a toilet. Each time he finds one, it appears to be functional, but when he tries to use it, it won't actually work.

Recurring dreams are a common phenomenon. In fact, Scripture contains several examples of repeated dreams or visions.

"Since the dream was given twice to Pharaoh, it means that the matter
has been determined by God, and he will carry it out soon."
~ Genesis 41:32

"Again, a second time, the voice said to him, 'What God has
made clean, do not call impure.' This happened three times,
and suddenly the object was taken up into heaven."
~ Acts 10:9-16

Why do we experience recurring dreams? The two passages above indicate that repeated dreams or visions serve to confirm that something is firmly established. Recurrent dreams often carry important messages, and the Lord uses repetition to ensure we grasp their significance. The dreams themselves can be either comforting or distressing, exhilarating or terrifying, instructive or confirming. Whatever the theme of the recurring dreams, it is the kindness of the Lord to remind us of a truth we've forgotten or isn't at the top of our mind.

From visions and trances to lucid dreams, visitations, and even déjà vu, it's clear that the Lord communicates in many ways during sleep and the moments surrounding it. These experiences can serve to open our understanding of the unseen realm. The Bible itself is filled with numerous examples of God using the night hours to reveal His will, provide guidance, and release creativity. Whether through recurring dreams or a sudden awareness of a presence, each encounter carries the potential to draw us closer to God and advance His purposes. As we grow in discernment and remain anchored in His Word, we can learn to embrace these encounters as moments to hear from Heaven.

> Recurrent dreams often carry important messages, and the Lord uses repetition to ensure we grasp their significance.

REFLECTIONS

1. What's the difference between a vision and a trance, and how might each one be used by God?

_____

_____

_____

2. Why do you think God sometimes speaks through visions or dreams rather than through direct communication?

_____

_____

_____

3. What role do you think angels play in our dreams and nighttime encounters?

_____

_____

_____

4. How might lucid dreaming be used by God for creative or spiritual purposes?

_____

_____

_____

5. Why do you think recurring dreams are often used to convey important messages or reminders?

_____

_____

_____

Chapter 16

TROUBLESHOOTING – DARK ENCOUNTERS WHILE SLEEPING

"I woke up in the middle of the night, pinned to my bed and unable to move or speak. A dark figure walked toward me with its arm outstretched, finger pointed at me. I was trying to say the name of Jesus but could only think it. The figure reached me and touched my finger with its finger. It disappeared and I was finally able to move." J.G.

Sleep Paralysis

Sleep paralysis is a condition while waking or falling asleep in which a person is aware but unable to move or speak. The person sees things that are normally unseen. This phenomenon is *from the enemy* and is designed to evoke fear and a sense of helplessness. Anyone who has experienced sleep paralysis will attest that it is, at the very least, disturbing and often deeply frightening. During a sleep paralysis episode, evil forces have a "captive audience" on which to impose their presence, taking advantage of the person's immobility and vulnerability. The dark presence can manifest in various ways, such as a visual apparition, a heavy weight pressing down on the body, or a pervasive sense of a menacing presence close by.

If you or someone you know experiences sleep paralysis, remember that you are not powerless. Call on the name of Jesus—if you can't speak out loud, cry out to Him in your mind. Keep pressing in until the oppression lifts. When you are free of the imposing presence, ask God to cleanse you, to wash you clean of the unclean atmosphere and of the fear. Be sure to appeal to God for justice for the violation.

> Sleep paralysis is *from the enemy* and is designed to invoke fear and a sense of helplessness.

Follow up by reaching out to a trusted believer and ask if they would be willing to join you in prayer over this situation. One of the enemy's strategies is to keep us trapped in secrecy and shame. But in Christ, shame has no place. We are citizens of God's Kingdom, a Kingdom filled with light and grace, where nothing is concealed.

"There is, therefore, now no condemnation for those who are in Christ Jesus."
~ Romans 8:1 ESV

"There is not one person who can hide their thoughts from God, for nothing that we do remains a secret, and nothing created is concealed, but everything is exposed and defenseless before his eyes, to whom we must render an account."
~ Hebrews 4:13 TPT

Ask the Holy Spirit if there is any reason the enemy might have access to torment. More on that below.

See / Sense / Hear a Menacing "Presence"

As in the previous chapter, many have experienced a presence when waking from sleep. Sometimes, this presence is evil. You may actually see its appearance. You may not see anything at all, but you can definitely feel its presence.

If the encounter is dark, command it to leave in the name of Jesus. Although potentially frightening, the feeling or appearance of this dark presence can give insight into the enemy's strategies. This is a great opportunity to leverage an intrusion against the enemy. Disempower its assignment in the name of Jesus. Declare God's truth in its place, ask God for justice, and as one of my prayer-warrior friends says, "Give the enemy a punch in the eye!"

Dark Encounters

Unfortunately, encounters with harmful forces can also occur. Once again, the enemy of our souls only has three moves in his playbook: to steal, kill, and destroy.[72] His agenda has not changed since the Garden of Eden. His tactics of deception and intimidation remain consistent. When it comes to sleep and dreaming, the enemy wants to derail us with terror, deception, or defilement.

As believers in Christ and born-again children of God, we have authority over the dark kingdom. Jesus won back the keys to death, hell, and the grave.

> *"When I saw him, I fell at his feet as if I were dead. But he laid his right hand on me and said, 'Don't be afraid! I am the First and the Last. I am the living one. I died but look—I am alive forever and ever! And I hold the keys of death and the grave.'"*
> ~ Revelation 1:18

It's no surprise that Jesus Himself is a primary example of these encounters. As the writer of Hebrews explains,

> *"For we do not have a high priest who cannot*
> *sympathize with our weaknesses,*
> *but **One who has been tempted in all things as we are**, yet without sin.*
> *Therefore, let us draw near with confidence to the throne of grace, so*
> *that we may receive mercy and find grace to help in time of need."*
> ~ Hebrews 4:15-16

During the forty days of fasting and praying, Jesus encountered both "the wild beasts," a metaphor for evil spirits, and, ultimately, satan attacking and attempting to entice Him. In each recorded encounter, the adversary was defeated through obedience to God and the Word of God.

> As believers in Christ and born-again children of God, we have authority over the dark kingdom.

Jesus declared that He gave us that same authority that He exercised to defeat evil forces. In this passage, snakes and scorpions are also metaphors for evil forces.

> *"Look, I have given you the authority to trample on snakes and scorpions*
> *and over all the power of the enemy; nothing at all will harm you."*
> ~ Luke 10:19

Paul, James, and Peter all wrote very pointedly about taking authority over demons. Paul lays out a multifaceted strategy for the Ephesians, with both defensive and offensive tools to defeat demons and dark authorities. Be strong in the Lord, put on the whole armor of God and stand against the schemes of the enemy, extinguish flaming arrows of the evil one with faith. He emphasizes "stand" or "withstand" three times in that short chapter.

*"...be strong in the Lord and in his mighty power. Put on the full armor of God, so that you can **take your stand** against the devil's schemes. For our struggle is not against flesh and blood, but against the rulers, against the authorities, against the powers of this dark world and against the spiritual forces of evil in the heavenly realms. Therefore, put on the full armor of God, so that when the day of evil comes, you may be able to **stand your ground**, and after you have done everything, to stand. **Stand firm then**, with the belt of truth buckled around your waist, with the breastplate of righteousness in place, and with your feet fitted with the readiness that comes from the gospel of peace. In addition to all this, take up the shield of faith, with which you can extinguish all the flaming arrows of the evil one. Take the helmet of salvation and the sword of the Spirit, which is the word of God. And pray in the Spirit on all occasions with all kinds of prayers and requests."*
~ Ephesians 6:10-18

James reveals several Kingdom keys in dealing with demonic encounters - "submission to God" and "resisting the enemy."

*"**Submit** yourselves, then, to God. **Resist** the devil, and he will flee from you."*
~ James 4:7

While asserting authority over evil intrusions, Peter echoes humility, submission to God, and resisting the devil.

*"**Humble** yourselves, therefore, **under God's mighty hand**, that He may lift you up in due time. Cast all your anxiety on Him because He cares for you. Be alert and of sober mind. Your enemy the devil prowls around like a roaring lion looking for someone to devour. **Resist** him, standing firm in the faith, because you know that the family of believers throughout the world is undergoing the same kind of sufferings. And the God of all grace, who called you to his eternal glory in Christ, after you have suffered a little while, will Himself restore you and make you strong, firm, and steadfast."*
~ 1 Peter 5: 6-10

These three passages reveal powerful tools, guaranteed to be effective in victory over temptation and demonic influence in everyday life and when confronted by an evil presence.

- Submit to God.
- Speak the Word of God.
- Stand firm.
- Resist the devil.
- Declare your authority because of the blood of Jesus and expel it.

Astral Projections

An astral projection is a *self-initiated* out of body experience. It is the *unclean* form of phenomenon described in the Scriptures, which is initiated by God. God can initiate a "translation," where He moves your spirit; a "transportation," where He moves your body; or a "being caught up," where He moves either your spirit or your physical body to the heavenly realm.[73] A person engaging in astral projection does so through occult or New Age practices, or by independently exploring the unseen realm. The objective is to acquire hidden knowledge,[74] manipulate others into sinful behavior, and exert supernatural influence or control over them.

Pride is the motivation in attempting to exert "power" over the unseen realm and over another person. Astral projections intrude to curse, to block destiny, and to incite fear.

What do you do if you encounter an astral projection? They have no power against prayer and the blood of Jesus. Take authority in Jesus' name, command it to leave, and forbid it to ever come again. Pray and ask the Father to assign angels to protect your home from supernatural intrusion. Speak the power of Jesus' blood over your home. Ask the Righteous Judge to hold the enemy accountable and give you justice for such an intrusion.

After asserting authority over a dark presence, again it's helpful to ask, "Why did this enter my home? Has something I've done, or something done by someone else in the home, opened a door for the enemy?"

The enemy does steal, kill, and destroy. He intrudes uninvited, not through the gate.[75] However sometimes doors are opened to harassment *through sin* – either ours or someone else's, or because of the atmospheres we've been in.

Protecting Yourself and Your Home

The dark forces that try to harass, deceive, and intimidate us were already defeated once and for all through the sinless life, death, burial, resurrection, and ascension of Jesus Christ. Even so, we continue to face their schemes. Here are just a few practical suggestions to protect yourself and your home.

Intentionally commit your home and property to the Lord putting yourself and all you hold dear under the blood of Jesus. Anoint the doorframes with oil asking for God's presence and protection over every part of your home. Saturate the atmosphere with worship. Gather with other believers in your home, filling the space with testimonies of God's goodness and the power of Scripture.[76] Let the praises and declarations of His faithfulness create a strong spiritual environment that invites His presence and protection.

Stay current in confession of sin and intentionally invite the Holy Spirit to search your heart.

"Search me, O God, and know my heart! Try me and know my thoughts!
And see if there be any grievous way in me and
lead me in the way everlasting!"
~ Psalm 139:23, 24

Ask the Holy Spirit to reveal any items in your home that are unholy and need to be removed and commit to disposing of them without delay. Pornographic material would fit that bill. Take a look through your belongings for anything with ties to the occult and get rid of it. Idols or statues used for worship by others are specifically forbidden in

Scripture. Likewise, items like Ouija boards, tarot cards, and horoscopes directly contradict biblical commands.

"You shall tear down their altars, smash their memorial stones, cut their Asherim to pieces, and burn their carved images in the fire. For you are a holy people to the Lord your God..."
~ Deuteronomy 7:5, 6a

One last suggestion is to "cleanse" before crossing the threshold of your home, apartment, or dorm. During her time as a missionary in Berlin, my niece Hannah would "cleanse" before crossing the threshold of her house after being out in different environments and atmospheres, some of them not so aligned with God's Kingdom. I've learned from her to do the same by simply stating, *"Anything not of the Kingdom of God that I've encountered today may not enter my home and has to leave now in Jesus' name."*

Nightmares

The fruit of the presence of the enemy is fear, torment, and deviation from our destiny. Nightmares are created by dark forces; forces set against the Kingdom of God. Their goal is to engender fear, harass, steal rest, and weaken a person. The enemy loves to steal the spotlight. He will employ any tactic to entice us to shift our focus away from God and onto him. After all, his chief original sin was pride and he and his kingdom have never changed their modus operandi.

> There are two ways in which the enemy influences our life - through sin or intrusion.

There are two ways in which the enemy influences our life – through sin or intrusion. As you read further, ask the Holy Spirit for revelation on why the enemy is having this influence.

Access Through Sin

If the access is through sin, it can stem from three sources –

1. My sin.
2. Sin in past generations.
3. Sin against me or trauma.

Here are steps to take to remove that access.

If the enemy's access is through my sin or sins in past generations, come out of agreement with the enemy by **confessing sin**.

> *"If we confess our sins, he is faithful and just and will forgive*
> *us our sins and purify us from all unrighteousness."*
> ~ 1 John 1:9

> *"Confess your sins to each other and pray for each other so that you may*
> *be healed. The prayer of a righteous person is powerful and effective."*
> ~ James 5:16

Follow confession with **repentance** either on your own behalf or on behalf of previous generations. Nehemiah provides a powerful example of this principle:

> *"Lord, the God of heaven, the great and awesome God, who keeps his*
> *covenant of love with those who love him and keep his commandments, let*
> *your ear be attentive and your eyes open to hear the prayer your servant is*
> *praying before you day and night for your servants, the people of Israel.* **I**
> **confess the sins we Israelites, including myself and my father's family,**
> **have committed against you.** *We have acted very wickedly toward you."*
> ~ Nehemiah 1:5-7

After confessing and repenting, the next step is to **renounce** the sin. To renounce simply means to state publicly that you no longer agree with a particular belief or that you will no longer behave in a particular way.

> *"The one who conceals his sins will not prosper, but whoever **confesses and renounces** them will find mercy."*
> ~ Proverbs 28:13

> To renounce simply means to state publicly that you no longer agree with a particular belief or that you will no longer behave in a particular way.

It's now crucial to **expel** any evil influence resulting from sin—whether it's your own or from previous generations. Command those forces to leave and go directly to Jesus for judgment.

Wrap it all up by **declaring God's truth** over your life. For every belief or action that contradicts the principles of God's Kingdom, there is an opposing truth. Ask the Lord to show you what that truth is. Research Scriptures that affirm that truth and **declare them over yourself and your home**.

> *"For the word of God is alive and active. Sharper than any double-edged sword, it penetrates even to dividing soul and spirit, joints and marrow; it judges the thoughts and attitudes of the heart."*
> ~ Hebrews 4:16

In summary, to eliminate access because of sin:

1. Confess
2. Repent
3. Renounce
4. Expel
5. Replace with Truth

Access Because of Sin Against Me

Nightmares also arise from sins committed against us and from trauma. As we discussed in Chapter 13, when it comes to nightmares, there *is* a cause and effect. Sins perpetrated on an individual and / or trauma they've experienced often manifest in nightmares. Repeated nightmares are like an "X" on a treasure map saying, "dig here!"

Although these nightmares are distressing, they act as a signal from the Lord that something requires attention and healing. God is never the source of sins against us, nor does He perpetrate trauma. But He is a Master at leveraging these grievous experiences to draw us into His healing heart of love *and* to catapult us into our destiny to an even greater measure. Joseph is a powerful example of this truth about God.

"You intended to harm me, but God intended it for good to accomplish what is now being done, the saving of many lives."
~ Genesis 50:20

Examples of trauma events that could cause nightmares include natural disasters, a violent attack or accident, military combat, sexual assault, physical abuse, the death of a loved one, bullying, severe illness, childhood neglect or abandonment, witnessing violence, or even sudden life changes. These events are particularly impactful when they are experienced by children.

If you are experiencing repeated nightmares and are aware of trauma in your life, ask the Holy Spirit to lead you to trustworthy, trauma-informed counsel. Commit yourself to the process of healing and sanctification, seeking comfort from the Holy Spirit and His perspective. [77]

If you are experiencing repeated nightmares and you're not consciously aware of any trauma, I encourage you to ask the Holy Spirit to bring to light any hidden hurts that need attention. Let the

Lord know you are willing to sort through what He reveals to you and partner with Him in your healing.

*"Search me, God, and know my heart; put me to the test and know my anxious thoughts; and see if there is **any hurtful way** in me and lead me in the everlasting way."*
~ Psalm 139:23-24

The Hebrew word for "hurtful way," *otseb*, also carries the meaning "pain – bodily or mental; sorrow." God is eager to work alongside us to heal hidden pain and sorrow and then lead us in "the way everlasting," or His life-giving ways.

Access Through Intrusion

Evil influence can also stem from external intrusions, not necessarily linked to sin. The enemy often interferes simply because he plays dirty. (I'm referring to an isolated nightmare, not a recurring pattern.) Sometimes this can occur because of dark ruling spirits in an area or region. Land in an area can be defiled in many ways including the shedding of innocent blood, witchcraft, and idol worship.

> For every belief or action that contradicts the principles of God's Kingdom, there is an opposing truth. Ask the Lord to show you what that truth is.

During a visit to Bavaria with family and missionary friends, I experienced a series of three intense nightmares in one night. I actually awoke from the third nightmare screaming. I got up in the middle of the night, took authority over the evil influence in Jesus' name and prayed cleansing over my mind, body, and spirit. The next morning when I woke, the others were already in the kitchen area of our air b&b. As I got dressed, I reflected on the nightmares thinking, *"Why didn't I call on the name of Jesus in my dream instead of just screaming?"* As I walked out of the bedroom to join the others, my bunk mate was just relating, *"She woke up screaming the name of Jesus!"* I was relieved to hear that I had called out the name of Jesus and made a mental note that sometimes we instinctively respond in our spirit without consciously knowing it! Later that week, we discovered that this particular area was known for its historical and current practice of witchcraft.

If the enemy has intruded, the solution is once again to take authority in Jesus' name. We have been bought with the blood of Jesus and given authority *over all the power of the enemy.*[78]

Such occasions are a strategic time to ask God for justice for this unlawful intrusion.

"Righteousness and justice are the foundation of your throne;
love and faithfulness go before you."
~ Psalm 89:14

"The Lord is our God, bringing justice everywhere on earth.
He will never forget His agreement or His promises, not in thousands of years."
~ Psalm 105:7, 8

Asking God for justice is a seldom-taught truth in Christian circles. Many believers I've encountered haven't realized that, as citizens of Heaven, we have the right to seek justice when the enemy infringes upon us.

Justice can come in many forms. We may witness an increase in favor; the loved one we've been praying for could come to know Jesus, we might experience breakthroughs in challenging situations, see financial prosperity or supernatural provision, or celebrate the restoration of a fractured relationship.

Joseph is a striking example of God's justice in the face of the injustices he endured throughout his life. Although he endured extreme highs and lows, he also experienced remarkable favor, developed in various areas of leadership and management, prospered financially beyond measure, and ultimately saw reconciliation with his family.

When you ask the Lord for justice, also ask Him to help you recognize it when it arrives. His justice may not come in the way you want or expect, but it will come.

Season of Soulish Dreams

When our soul more predominantly rules over our spirit, repeated soul dreams can occur. To review, soul dreams can be chaotic, leave us frustrated or yearning for something that is a fleshly desire. They can highlight insecurities and fears. The colors in these dreams are often muted.

Many of us have spent much of our lives with our mind, will, and emotions – the soul – in the driver seat. It's no wonder. What we see, hear, and feel in the natural world can easily overwhelm our senses and appear more real than the things that are unseen. These realities captivate our attention and consequently influence our dreams.

Our spirits were designed to rule over our soul, which in turn rules over our body. This flow of authority—spirit over soul, and soul over body—enables a life marked by God's fruitfulness.

"If we walk by the spirit, we will not carry out the desires of the flesh."[79]

"May your whole spirit, soul and body be kept blameless
at the coming of our Lord Jesus Christ."
~ 1 Thessalonians 5:23

Ecclesiastes tells us that troubled dreams arise from a mind distracted and weighed down with too much business in the day.

> Our spirits were designed to rule over our soul, which in turn rules over our body.

"A dream comes when there are many cares" (Ecclesiastes 5:3). Or as the Legacy Standard Bible translates, *"For the dream comes through abundant endeavor..."*

Soul dreams stem from excessive worry about

tasks. Over commitment. Trying to accomplish too much. Psalm 127:2 has been a verse frequently quoted in our home over the years.

"It is vain for you to rise up early, to retire late,
to eat the bread of painful labors;
for He gives to His beloved even in his sleep."

Contrast this troubled sleep with the restful sleep of someone who has worked industriously, as described in Ecclesiastes 5:12, *"...The sleep of the laborer is sweet, whether he eats little or much."* We were designed to work six days a week and rest on the seventh. An industrious lifestyle, physical exercise, and intentional partnership with the Father in the *"good works which He prepared beforehand,"*[80] paired with regular periods of rest, create a conducive atmosphere for sweet sleep.

Psalm 127:2, above, is consistent with the concept of soul dreams, or *"...dreams which you cause to be dreamed"* (Jeremiah 29:8). If this is a pattern, it's a good indication that self-will rules over the spirit in a person's life. Once again, Psalm 131 serves as a powerful remedy for distressing dreams that arise from relying on our own soul.

"Lord, my heart is not proud, my eyes are not haughty.
I don't concern myself with matters too great or too awesome for me to grasp.
Instead, I have calmed and quieted myself, like a weaned child
who no longer cries for its mother's milk.
Yes, like a weaned child is my soul within me."

If you are experiencing a lot of soulish dreams, intentionally focus on strengthening your spirit. Here are several ways Scripture encourages us to strengthen and build up our spirit:

- **Feed on the Word of God** – Hebrews 4:12 *"For the word of God is living and powerful, and sharper than any two-edged sword, piercing even to the **division of soul and spirit**, and of joints and marrow, and is a discerner of the thoughts and intents of the heart."*

- **Worship** - John 4:24 *"God is Spirit, and those who worship Him must worship in spirit and truth."*
- **Pray** - Ephesians 6:18 *"...praying at all times in the Spirit, with all prayer and supplication."*
- **Obedience**- John 4:34 *Jesus said to them, "My food is to do the will of Him who sent Me, and to finish His work."*
- **Speak in Tongues** - 1 Corinthians 14:4, 5 *"The one who speaks in a tongue **builds up himself** but the one who prophesies builds up the church. Now I want you all to speak in tongues, but even more to prophesy."*
- **Confess Envy Or Unforgiveness** - Galatians 5:25, 26 *If we live by the Spirit, let us also keep in step with the Spirit. Let us not become conceited, provoking one another, **envying one another.**"*
- **Do Stuff That Makes Your Spirit Come Alive** - Discover how God uniquely designed you to "come alive" spiritually. Leverage those activities. When do you frequently "feel inspired" or "hear from God"?

Another suggestion when having soulish or dark dreams is to take a look at your bedtime routine. Are you cultivating an atmosphere of peace before going to sleep? Reducing TV and screen time can really help, as the constant flow of images from movies and shows can overwhelm our ability to receive from the Lord. Excessive alcohol can also fragment sleep, leading to interruptions in our dreams.

I've found that making a focused effort to set aside worries and concerns for myself and others makes a huge difference. Focus on the Lord, His Presence of shalom, His love. Rest in all that God's covenant with us provides - belonging, comradery, healing, joy, protection, comfort. Thank Him for watching over you, telling Him you are eager to hear from Him in the night. Ask the Father what is on His heart and meditate on that.

Emotional Hangover From a Dream

Dreams evoke a full range of emotions and sometimes intense emotion. Remember that dreams are crafted to exaggerate elements for emphasis, sort of a "Hey, look at me!" effect. Because dreams are inherently elusive, making it difficult not only to remember them but also to grasp the message contained within them, the Lord allows the emotional impact to help us hang on to the message of the dream.

"Then I, Daniel, was overcome and lay sick for several days. Afterward I got up and performed my duties for the king, but I was greatly troubled by the vision and could not understand it."
~ Daniel 8:27

"While he was sitting on the judgment seat, his wife sent to him, saying, 'Have nothing to do with that just Man, for I have suffered many things today in a dream because of Him.'"
~ Matthew 27:19

When a dream leaves you with an emotional hangover, taking certain steps can help to restore peace and fortitude. Both Daniel and Pilate's wife were emotionally hungover as a result of a dream from God. Go to the Father for the comfort found in His Presence, calming our overwrought nerves. Just being in His Presence alone can soothe our troubled emotions and flood us with a deep sense of "home." Play worship music and read the Word, washing your soul from agitation. When a dream from the enemy evokes a powerful emotional reaction, take authority over evil in Jesus' name and flip the dream, declaring God's perspective over the content of the experience.

In either case, ask the Holy Spirit for greater understanding and the wisdom to apply what He is showing you. If the dream is from the Lord, thank Him for speaking in your dream.

Although the encounters and phenomena in this chapter may be intense and unsettling, God is with us. We are not alone.[81] He wants us to be free and thriving even more than we do. Keep seeking freedom from dark encounters. It is possible – I'm living proof.

REFLECTIONS

1. Have you or someone you know ever experienced sleep paralysis, and how did you respond in that moment? How can you respond in the moment, and what are some steps you can take to shield yourself from these intrusions?

_____

_____

_____

2. How can you identify areas in your life where you might be unknowingly giving the enemy access, and what steps can you take to close those doors?

_____

_____

_____

3. What specific prayers or declarations have helped you find peace and protection in your home or personal space, especially if you've experienced dark encounters during the night?

_____

_____

_____

4. Have you ever considered appealing to God for justice after spiritual violations? What would it look like for you to call on God's justice in your life when you feel spiritually violated, whether through nightmares, astral projection, or other attacks?

_____

_____

_____

5. What are some practical changes you can make in your nightly routine to ensure that you're mentally and spiritually prepared for a restful night free from fear or unsettling dreams?

_____

_____

_____

Chapter 17

WHEN YOU ARE MET WITH RESISTANCE

"All truth passes through three stages.
First, it is ridiculed.
Second, it is violently opposed.
Third, it is accepted as being self-evident."
~ Aurthur Schaupenhauer

Being met with resistance is an all too familiar experience when it comes to biblical dream interpretation in the Western Church. These are just a few of the objections I've heard while discussing or teaching dream interpretation from a biblical perspective.

"There's no biblical example of studying dream interpretation."
"Dream interpretation is New Age and demonic."
"So, are you saying you think every dream is from God?"
"We don't need dreams; we have the written word of God."
"I don't need to study dream interpretation - I just ask God, and He tells me what it means."
"You know, sometimes a dream is just a dream."

And if not met with outright resistance, God speaking through dreams is regarded as unnecessary for "us" but, of course, could be useful in other parts of the world. You know, for those people who really need it. *"Have you heard that Muslims are having dreams of Jesus?!"* is often the only touchpoint of reference many Western Christians offer when this topic is brought up. Don't get me wrong; Muslims meeting Jesus in dreams is absolutely phenomenal. I praise God for this. The point is, somehow, the personal relevance of dreams is often considered disconnected from our everyday reality.

Once again, in our Greek-influenced culture, the recognition of dreams as a significant part of our walk with Jesus has been almost entirely absent in mainstream denominations. So, the lack of relatability is completely understandable.

Keeping in mind that dream interpretation is still largely considered suspect in many Christian circles, if you do embrace this gift from the Father, it's helpful to prepare your heart for some pushback. It is likely that we will encounter resistance when we are sharing a dream, referring to dream interpretation, or even talking about dreams in general. When this happens, it's easy to respond inwardly with defensiveness or anxiety.

But remember, it's not about you.

I have found it helpful to remind myself of how I used to be resistant to dream interpretation as well as many other biblically based realities of the Spirit. I was a classic case of "contempt prior to investigation!" I had wrongly assumed that simply agreeing with the teachings I received was enough to replace doing my own investigation. Did I realize that's what I was doing? No. Could I still be operating this way in some areas of my life? Absolutely, yes.

One of the wisest questions to ask ourselves before the Lord is, "What if I'm wrong?" It's important to regularly examine, in the light of Scripture, what we believe about God, ourselves, and the world around us. Jesus' rebuke of the Sadducees offers us an opportunity to reflect on our own condition,

"You are mistaken, since you do not understand
the Scriptures nor the power of God."
~ Matthew 22:29

When faced with resistance, it's important to remember where we came from and stay in a place of peace. Simply put, those who resist us have their own feelings, and their perspective today may not be the same a year from now. After all, aren't we all in a process of transformation?

Unfortunately, among many earnest believers who study and honor the Word of God, there is a widespread fear of "being deceived." Paul did warn us not to be deceived by false teachings, empty philosophies, sinful influences, or anything that distorts the truth of the gospel.[82] That's not what I'm talking about. This isn't an issue of false doctrine—it's about fear or discomfort around a biblical pattern of how God has regularly chosen to speak to humanity.

As I shared in Chapter 2, fear and assumptions can create barriers that inhibit us from fully embracing the profound and transformative aspects of God's ways.

"'For My thoughts are not your thoughts, nor are your ways My ways,'
declares the LORD. 'For as the heavens are higher than the earth, so are
My ways higher than your ways and My thoughts than your thoughts.'"
~ Isaiah 55:8, 9

John Paul Jackson coined the phrase, *"Peace is the potting soil for revelation."* Staying rooted in shalom is crucial when considering new paradigms. One approach I've used to help ease fear when teaching dream interpretation courses is to ask the group for a show of hands as I ask this question: *"How many of you understand something about the Lord and your walk with Him today that you didn't know five years ago?"* Every hand goes up.

I then follow up with, *"So were you **deceived**?"* Often, uncertainty registers on their faces, and their hands gradually go down. At this point, I continue, *"I mean, you weren't aware of the truth you are living in now, right? Your thinking was flawed in some aspect.*

"Here's the reality: we all have limited understanding, and the Holy Spirit is in the process of leading and guiding us into all truth. We are in a process. He is faithful! Even if we do legitimately fall into deception, we can trust Him to lead us out. We surround ourselves with mature believers. We saturate ourselves with the Word of God. We can relax, stay close to Him, and keep our hearts open to whatever He might be showing us."

The biblical reality remains that dreams carry incredible transformative potential in the dreamer's life and even for the lives around them. A quick glance at dreams recorded in Scripture will attest to this – nations saved from starvation, a business catalyzed, the Messiah saved from premature death. I have personally witnessed the healing, guiding, eye-opening, and even life-changing effects when God reveals the interpretation of a dream.

Considering the potential for true transformation, I believe it's absolutely worth facing some resistance, criticism, or even rejection if it means reaching and helping someone. They may find hope for a prodigal, healing for an insecurity, correction for a destructive mindset, or direction for their future. Many times over, I've seen tears of relief when the Holy Spirit reveals the message of a dream. The risk is worth the reward.

Often, what we don't understand or are unfamiliar with can trigger fear. Reactions and resistance arise when what you're sharing challenges their current understanding of God. And that's okay! If you face opposition, trust that the Lord is with you to guide the conversation. Ask the Holy Spirit, "Is this a fruitful conversation at this time?" It may simply not be the right time for them to receive. Our goal in sharing is to serve them, not to convince them.

My father-in law graduated to heaven several years ago, leaving behind a rich reservoir of wisdom. I've found one of his insights to be particularly valuable when navigating interactions with individuals who see things differently than I do.

"There are three levels of belief:

> *Opinion*
> *Conviction*
> *Doctrine*

Opinions are fluid, changeable, and a dime a dozen. Convictions are fewer, stronger, more thought through. Doctrine is normative for all believers in every culture or language. We don't impose our opinions or convictions on other people. But doctrine is what you die for."[84]

In my own experience and in observing others, I've noticed how easily we can elevate *opinions* to the *conviction* category, and our *convictions* to the level of *doctrine.* This can lead to a world of trouble when it comes to relating to brothers and sisters who have differing perspectives. Pay close attention to your own internal reaction when you bump up against resistance. Frustration and judgmental attitudes are great flags to help us recognize where we are wanting to *impose our convictions* on someone else.

> Frustration and judgmental attitudes are great flags to help us recognize where we are wanting to *impose our convictions* on someone else.

The goal is to keep our own heart clear of expectations and resentments. Honor them in their perspective no matter how different it is from yours. You don't have to agree with their current understanding to treat them with the *respect* due to a fellow servant of Jesus.

After all, don't we also feel strongly about our convictions?

The main truth I strive to remember when met with resistance is that the other person is the Lord's servant, and God is responsible for their life and understanding. They belong to Him.

> *"...It is the glory of God to conceal a matter, but*
> *it is the glory of kings to search it out!"*
> ~ Proverbs 25:2

REFLECTIONS

1. How do you personally handle resistance when introducing biblical dream interpretation or other unfamiliar scriptural realities to others?

_____

_____

_____

2. How can we differentiate between opinions, convictions, and doctrines in our discussions with others?

_____

_____

_____

3. How do you stay rooted in peace ("shalom") when presenting a concept that challenges someone's understanding?

_____

_____

_____

4. Why is it important to ask ourselves, "What if I'm wrong?" in relation to our beliefs about God and His ways?

_____

_____

_____

5. Can you think of a time when your understanding of a spiritual matter changed? How did it affect your walk with God?

_____

_____

_____

Chapter 18

DON'T GO IT ALONE

*"I was thanking the Lord for our community and was thinking how
important it is to have a group that carries the heart of the Father
and chooses to be for one another. Sharing dreams can lead us into
some vulnerable spaces and it is such a gift to know that you will be
met with hope and encouragement and not gossip or judgment. Find
those kinds of people and learn to be that person for others!"*
~ Nicole P. from our Dream Community

*"At this, Daniel went into the king and asked for time, so that he might
interpret the dream for him. Then Daniel returned to his house and explained
the matter to his friends Hananiah, Mishael and Azariah. He urged them
to plead for mercy from the God of heaven concerning this mystery, so that
he and his friends might not be executed with the rest of the wise men of
Babylon. During the night the mystery was revealed to Daniel in a vision.*

'Praise be to the name of God for ever and ever...
He gives wisdom to the wise
and knowledge to the discerning.
He reveals deep and hidden things;

he knows what lies in darkness,
and light dwells with him.
...you have made known to me what we asked of you,
you have made known to us the dream of the king.'"
~ Daniel 2:16-23

At the time of writing this, I had just wrapped up a Zoom call focused on prayer and planning for an upcoming retreat. While we were praying and strategizing, I suddenly remembered a dream that I'd had two days earlier which involved the retreat leader. Although I had written the dream down, the dream only came to life *in the company of these friends*! I hadn't received anything close to full revelation on the dream, and as I shared it, the other team members gained numerous insights that I had overlooked. To be honest, it wasn't until I brought it up that I even realized the dream was related to the retreat. Through that dream, the Lord gave us strategic intel and encouragement for the team, and particularly for the leader.

"He makes the whole body fit together perfectly. As each part
does its own special work, it helps the other parts grow, so that
the whole body is healthy and growing and full of love."
~ Ephesians 4:16

I'm assuming that if you've made it this far in the book, it's likely you are wanting to grow in understanding and stewarding dreams. Just like any other area of life, trying to navigate dream interpretation on our own can be slow-going with limited results. The reality is, we were never meant to do this alone. We need each other. And God, in His wisdom, wants it that way. After all, He's the one who set the whole system up.

This translation of the well-known passage in Hebrews really resonates with me...

*"And let us consider each other carefully for the purpose of sparking
love and good deeds. Don't stop meeting together with other believers,
which some people have gotten into the habit of doing. Instead,
encourage each other, especially as you see the day drawing near."*
~ Hebrews 10:24-25 (CEB)

"Sparking" is exactly what happens when collaborating in the realm
of dreams. Time after time, we have witnessed the joy in our community
when the mystery of a dream takes shape and becomes clear as we work
on it together.

Ask God for a Dream Community

What steps can you take to ensure that
you are not "going it alone" as you grow in
God's gift of dreams? Our experience has
shown us that cultivating a healthy dream
community typically requires intentional,
humble, persistent effort. A network like
this doesn't "just happen." The first concrete
step in developing a dream culture is simply to ask God for it. And keep
asking. Jesus promises,

> Cultivating a healthy
> dream community typically
> requires intentional,
> humble, persistent effort.

*"Ask and it will be given to you; seek and you will find; knock and the
door will be opened to you. For everyone who asks receives; the one who
seeks finds; and to the one who knocks, the door will be opened."*
~ Matthew 7:7-8

Although it may not happen overnight, it *will* come.

*"...How gracious He will be when you cry for help! As soon as He hears,
He will answer you. Although the Lord gives you the bread of adversity and
the water of affliction, your teachers will be hidden no more; with your own*

eyes you will see them. Whether you turn to the right or to the left, your
ears will hear a voice behind you, saying, 'This is the way; walk in it.'"
~ Isaiah 30: 19-21

Do Whatever It Takes

No church or ministry has the vision or expertise to cover *every* area of life in Christ. As you seek a community of like-minded believers, you may need to venture beyond your current circles to find "your people." This doesn't mean abandoning your community but rather expanding your growth by connecting with others who can help sharpen and stretch you. Just like when preparing a gourmet meal, no one thinks twice about visiting a specialty store for unique ingredients or taking a cooking class to hone skills. Similarly, most encourage attending a conference or learning from a gifted teacher as an essential ingredient in your spiritual development.

This was certainly true in my case. I made a deliberate decision to show up in places where people were functioning in the ways I knew were available, but not yet a reality in my own experience. I invested financially to attend conferences and trainings. We had young children at the time and being gone for a weekend was costly for both my husband and for me.

I was so hungry that I often attended gatherings where I knew no one. It helped that I already had a solid community as an anchor. Even though I felt alone among these strangers, I dove in, engaged fully, and practiced. I learned to embrace making mistakes and looking foolish, trusting that growth would come through trial and error. Through this process, I believed I would experience firsthand the transformative power of dreams and their interpretation, even though the process was uncomfortable at times. These sacrifices of time, money, comfort, and effort paid off more profoundly than I had thought possible. As John

Paul Jackson wisely remarked, *"You find out where God is taking you by the quality of the people He brings around you."*[85]

Be open to taking risks. Commit to investing the time. Take fear off the table and be confident that God will lead you and protect you as you explore. He always gives back way more than what we offer Him.

Develop Interpretation Skills Together

Developing interpretation skills with a group of like-minded believers is incredibly effective. Once you find others who are passionate about stewarding dreams, be intentional about growing together. Early on in building our dream community, one of our members set up a Voxer group where we could share dreams and offer feedback to one another. This proved to be remarkably effective. (Any walkie-talkie, or video app such as Marco Polo works just as well.) Gathering frequently or even hopping on the phone to work through dreams just wasn't realistic with busy schedules. This way we were able to create a collective record of dreams, gain insight from each other, develop a lens for symbolism, and most of all —practice, practice, practice!

Resources for biblical dream interpretation are invaluable.[86] I'm not talking about plugging your dream into some resource or algorithm to spit out an interpretation. I'm referring to an encyclopedia of biblical imagery, or common dream symbols and possible meanings with scriptural references, or materials that help metaphorical thinking through a biblical lens. Everyone in our community has invested in these. Frequently, one of us will send a text to the group while they are away from home requesting someone to look up the biblical imagery for a certain dream element, color, or number. If a casual observer were to read some of these texts, they'd be scratching their heads.

"What does a narwal mean?"

"A walrus was jogging with me. Any thoughts?"

"What's the color red represent again?"

"Can someone send me the Hebrew meaning of the number 11?"

And of course, the ultimate resource is the Word of God. It's our foundation and the ultimate guide for understanding dreams, by revelation of the Holy Spirit.

Keep investing in your understanding of God's ways and how He communicates. Take online or in-person courses, like those offered by Streams Ministries or through our ministry, to deepen your knowledge. You don't have to do it alone - why not study with a friend or a church group? Immersing yourself in a community focused on growing in dream interpretation will create a synergy that accelerates your progress and enriches the lives of those around you. As you continue on this journey, keep inviting others to join you in learning to listen to the Lord through the dreams He gives.

Make Dreams a Part of Everyday Conversation!

Keep sharing about dreams and the power of their interpretations. For me, the concept of biblical dream interpretation didn't really click until someone else introduced it. That moment opened my eyes, and the gift of that insight has been life changing. It's amazing what happens when dreams and their meanings are brought into conversation—it sparks curiosity, opens doors for deeper understanding, and creates opportunities for meaningful connections.

Here's an encouraging encounter from a good friend:

> *"At the grocery store, I shared with the cashier that I was taking dream interpretation classes, and I asked if she had a dream. She lit up and said, "Yes! I keep having the same dream over and over, and I have wondered what it means! In the dream, a kind man is pursuing me and wants to marry me!*
>
> *"I instantly had revelation from the Holy Spirit that God had been pursuing her and was revealing it to her in her dreams. I told her: That's a great dream! It means that God is pursuing*

you and wants to have a relationship with you, and that He is kind.' She seemed genuinely touched by this and heartily thanked me."

Anything new can feel a bit awkward or uncomfortable at first. Dreams, in particular, aren't something most people openly talk about—unless it's to say, "I had the craziest dream...!" But simply bringing them into regular conversation helps normalize the topic and can make others feel more at ease. When you mention how you explore their possible meaning through biblical imagery and praying for interpretation, people often feel more comfortable sharing their own dreams and experiences.

I rarely come across disinterest when I bring up dream interpretation. In fact, the opposite is true - people are usually excited to talk about their dreams. They're eager to understand them better. So, I encourage you to weave conversations about dreams into your everyday interactions. – at the breakfast table, or at the supermarket, or at the gym, at your Christmas party, at your kid's soccer game.

Protocol in the Dream Community

As you cultivate a healthy community for dream interpretation, keep looking for the gold in one another. Operate in the protocol of love. A large part of protocol revolves around the tongue. James says no one can tame it[87]—and that's accurate. But the Holy Spirit can! He embodies perfect love and perfect self-control. How we say what we say really does matter.

If we truly want to foster a safe space that promotes risk-taking and growth, we also need to let go of the urge to correct every mistake. This is especially important in sincere, Bible-centered evangelical communities, where there's often a hair-trigger response to correct even the smallest nuances in someone else's theology or wording. It doesn't really require a spiritual gift to point out what's wrong with someone else. On the contrary, it takes much more maturity to recognize God's good plans in them and draw that out.

Much of how we communicate is cultural – from our upbringing and how we've learned to communicate in particular communities. Every family and every group develops its own "language"; a signature way of interacting. And, without realizing it, some of that language can end up being controlling and defining.

Ever find yourself on the receiving end of one of these scenarios?

- You're criticized for your word choice instead of the other person listening to the heart behind what you're saying.
- Being told what you "should" do or "need" to do.
- You confide in a friend and they "share" it as a prayer request with others.
- In front of others, you're asked to share your experience – "Bob, I know you've really struggled with your temper...tell us what you have learned through that?"
- Being asked probing or personal questions.
- You confront someone for crossing a boundary, and the response is something like, "Well, I guess you don't want me speaking into your life..."
- You're connected to someone influential, and people attempt to access them by going through you.
- Scripture is used to manipulate and guilt-trip.
- You're invited for coffee, only to find out it's actually a setup for a drive-by confrontation.
- After offering your perspective, you hear, "Oh, you must be a _____,". (fill in any theological label du jour.)

Most of us have been at the receiving end of these behaviors. Even more importantly, have you ever found *yourself* engaging in these behaviors? I can say I've been guilty of most of these at one time or another!

Here are a few phrases we've found helpful to adopt:

Rather than...	Try instead...
"You should / you need to..."	"Have you considered..."
Unsolicited advice...	"Did they ask?"
"Here's what I think..."	"I have some thoughts if you're interested."
Probing questions...	Do I really need to know?
Sharing someone else's story	Share your own experience
Giving my opinion...	Ask questions instead
Labeling someone's beliefs	See them as an individual

Another tool to evaluate before speaking is the acronym, THINK. Is what I'm about to say,

T - Thoughtful

H - Helpful

I - In Season

N - Necessary

K - Kind

Our experience has been that it takes concerted focus to change these patterns of relating. Pausing to find the right way to phrase something can feel a bit awkward. But the fruit is invaluable – good will within the community, lack of fear in conversations, even laughter when we mess up. It's definitely worth the effort and practice!

I hope the following testimonials and practical tips from our dream community encourage you. Receiving them certainly encouraged me.

Testimonials from Our Community

Nicole P.

"Learning about biblical dream interpretation and finding others like me was such a big deal. People don't think I'm crazy. It brought meaning to some of the chaos that I grew up with in the area of dreams and seeing. It has opened me up to long for more.

"In a community, hearing of other's dreams ignites yearning for more. Encourages me to pray more earnestly for God dreams. For instance, a woman in our small group shared a dream pointing to revival. We springboarded off of this for group edification and to pray together. We refrain from saying 'thus saith the Lord,' communicating in non-usurping ways.

"Some parameters are good, like symbolism books, but they are not always right. We are using these tools and relying on the Holy Spirit. I find it's helpful to have others hear our own dreams because we can make assumptions about our own dreams and others can sometimes see more objectively. Dreams can be emotionally charged, and others are more removed. We're learning to be strong enough to hear a dream and call out what needs to be called out.

"Even if you don't dream a lot, learning about dream interpretation is important. Doesn't mean it's not relevant in your community. There's no shame in not being the 'dreamer!' It's important to have a safe place to be vulnerable and to process our dreams. There's no shame around the content of our dreams."

Lori M.

"When I was new to dream interpretation, I valued my dream community for the purpose of learning and growing in interpretation skills. It was encouraging and insightful to share a dream or hear a dream, and work on its interpretation with another individual or a group. The synergy was motivating, helpful, and enjoyable.

"Now with mature skills, I value dream communities for intercession. On a local, personal level, I find great benefit in sharing my personal dreams with trusted friends to gain wisdom for my life and pray into situations. And of course, it's reciprocal, I share my dream insights and prayer strategies for dreamer friends.

"On a national and international level, I partner in intercession with seasoned communities that seek the Lord for his strategies, expecting Him to answer through dreams. The group interprets the dreams corporately which builds unity and unlocks the dream mysteries. Each member has a contribution, and I find it awe-inspiring to witness the heavenly message unfold. In these intercession groups, we dream, we fast and pray, then we watch the newspapers."

Amy L.

"Learning about dream interpretation has been a huge thing in my life. Processing dreams in a safe community provided consistency, great feedback, and learning cues for me. When we started, three of us shared our dreams on a Voxer Line. It provided a record for me to go back to. When we did this in community, not only did I have a record of my dreams, but others had a record of my dreams. They would remember my dreams helping me to string pearls together that formed a bigger story. We discovered Scriptures that correlate with the dreams.

"Even today, being in community for a long time, we remember each other's dreams, 'Oh that's just like your dream' or 'just like the dream I had that you were in.' This is vital for people to thrive, especially in the early days. It keeps you motivated and going! A dream community brings things into focus: what has happened in the past, what is taking place in the present, and what the Lord is leading us to in the future, what the Spirit is giving in that community – It's just a beautiful dance. I have always loved it and it's something that is not as vibrant right now in my life and I miss it. I really miss it.

"I learned so much both from the seasoned ones in the gifts and those that are youngins', because we all hear from the Holy Spirit differently. We can push and ask great questions and just practice, practice, practice – seeing what falls, what is picked up, what lands really well, and what's just put on the shelf. It's such a great environment for practicing discernment within a group. I received encouragement on how I filtered things, the way that others developed my sense of self in Jesus, the way that other people filter things. It developed my sense of self and character in the Lord. The true self in Jesus, not just kind of what I thought about myself. I encourage you to get in a group of two or three. A cord of three is not easily broken!"

Kristofer W.

"Every gift of the spirit is best stewarded and grown in the context of community. So *'stir up the gift'* 2 Timothy 1:16 as we *'Spur one another on …'* Hebrews 10:24.

"As we found kindred spirits with a passion for prayer and stirring up the gifts, we grew in faith and our spiritual gifts. All because the bonds of friendship grow, as the spirit weaves and knits your hearts together in love (Colossians 2:2). If you are searching for 'Your people', you will find them where hunger meets hunger for the things of God.

"Yes, it will probably be messy. Yes, there will be questions with no immediate answers. Yes, there should be uncomfortable tension because healthy things grow, and growing things change, as we are transformed by the renewing of our minds in the safe setting of a family on mission. And yes, it's worth it!"

Bonnie H.

"Throughout my childhood, I had nightmares. Even though I knew God spoke through dreams, I would pray every night not to dream. It felt too risky to trust God with my dream life. At some point, I stopped praying not to dream and began remembering my dreams and writing them down. The nightmares didn't return, and I was grateful, but it wasn't until I began to study biblical dream interpretation with Kathy Gray that I really began to value dreams as a way to deepen my intimacy with Jesus.

"There are many times when I am puzzled about what certain elements in my dreams mean. Yes, there are books that can help with this, but they are only guides and not applicable for every dream. So even though the dream is mine -and might be about me or my family-the Holy Spirit often nudges me to bring others into the mix. This is when working through dreams with a group of friends is so valuable. It's like we're all working on a jigsaw puzzle together each of us contributing pieces until the whole picture comes into view. Not only do I benefit with more clarity about my dream, but the entire group learns from one another. We are all practicing this and don't always get it right, but it is a safe space for us to share and offer up what we feel, the Holy Spirit is saying."

"As iron sharpens iron, so a friend sharpens a friend."
~ Proverbs 27:17 NLT

Karen B.

"Being part of a dream community has been key to expanding my knowledge and understanding and practice. I think for me one of the specific experiences has been truly understanding that God speaks through dreams. Even the dreams that seem scary can be helpful and actually have good direction! My experience has been that unless you are actively participating and practicing dreams and interpretation, you won't grow nearly as quickly."

Jean Pierre G.

"Becoming part of a dream community was a huge one for me. When my wife and I first started dating, she happened to get my dream book where I was writing all of my nightmares, (because that's all I had before Jesus), and it almost ended our relationship because of all the visual things that I saw day in and day out. Ever since I was a little kid in New Orleans, I had evil night terrors. I remember telling people like my mom, dad, and sister, but they thought I was a freak because I would wake up sweaty and screaming at the top of my lungs with scratches and bruises and welts all over my body. They would make me go see a psychiatrist thinking that I was doing bodily damage to myself, but it was never me. I was having night terrors and now I know I was being attacked every night.

"I didn't know what to do, so as the years went by, I just learned how to deal with it - just going to bed not sleeping, hoping not to sleep, just hoping it's not as bad as the night before. I was always so scared to go to sleep that later in my teens and in my 20s and 30s I would take stuff to keep myself awake. I acted tough, but the second I laid in bed I would be so scared to go to sleep. I remember so many times even before I was a believer, I would pray and pray that I would not dream anything. I didn't want good dreams, I didn't want bad dreams, I didn't want anything - I just wanted to sleep and I could never sleep. When you dream like that at night for such a long period of time, you start to think that you're crazy. It got to a point where I couldn't tell what was real and what was just in my nightmares.

"Once I found Jesus, I don't think I've had a nightmare since! It's amazing because once I said yes to Jesus, all I've had since then are super poetic dreams just filled with color, and the enemy doesn't have anything on me anymore! I didn't know anyone else who dreamed like me, so I never talked about it. Having other people around me that are dreamers is so beneficial. When I went to the dream workshop, I knew my dreams were more elaborate than the people at that workshop but finally finding that I'm not an outlier in this area being a believer was huge!"

Kris & Ashley W.

"One time when we were on the prayer team together, no one came in for prayer, so we sat around and talked. I shared that I had a dream that was really profound and involved my brother. Ashley and I knew dreams had meaning, but we had no Holy blueprint for figuring out what it could be.

"Kathy asked if I'd like to share the dream aloud. I did, and afterwards Kathy had profound insight & revelation! We were like, 'how did you do that?' And she introduced us to John Paul Jackson, Streams Ministries, her story - it was a catalyst for biblical dream interpretation!"

Lisa T.

"God loves unity and has a remarkable way of using dreams to communicate with us in powerful and profound ways. Through the dreams, visions and messages He imparts while we sleep, He is able to reveal His will, offer guidance, and even provide glimpses into the spiritual realm. As I have opened myself up to receiving these divine dreams, I have been amazed at how they have breathed new life into the scriptural accounts of God speaking through dreams. Suddenly, passages that once felt distant have become alive and personally meaningful, resonating with the intimate experiences I've had of the Lord using this unique mode of communication. This supernatural dimension to my walk with God has had a transformative effect, deepening my faith, expanding my understanding, and strengthening my relationship with the Lord in ways I never could have anticipated. I am forever grateful for how God chooses to speak to me through the conduit of dreams."

Tara W.

"My very active dream life since childhood has always been so interesting, but also frustrating. What did all these dreams mean? I was prophesied over in eighth grade that I would be a prophetic dreamer and that there would be people to help me interpret them.

"As dreams came up in my teens and early adulthood, I was at a loss to know how to understand them. I was able to find resources on my own (namely John Paul Jackson recordings and books) which helped a great deal. However, I often felt stumped by many of my dreams.

"In recent years, the dreaming has amped up a great deal! (For reference, I have over 500 dreams in my phone just from the last seven years.) In the last year, the Lord led me to a wonderful community of fellow dreamers. When I first was introduced and attended my first class, I was ecstatic to find others who were as passionate. I felt my spirit sigh in relief and have since found others to share my dreams with and receive help in hearing what the Lord is saying without my logic and biases to cloud them. I'm growing in understanding, and I'm also able to practice in a safe space with others learning alongside me. It's been one of the greatest blessings in the last year.

"Practically, I've found it vital to be vulnerable and share dreams that are even embarrassing at times. Once I began to do so and received understanding and sincere responses, I felt safe to continue to share. I also find it vital to hold everything loosely in an open hand. If someone doesn't have revelation, I find comfort in knowing that the Lord will show me at another time or wants to reveal it to me another way. I find that although the interpretation is a goal, the connection and unity that comes from seeking it with others is just as life-giving.

"I've found it most helpful to record my dreams digitally, so I can search back in them quickly. I also find that I can have an extremely detailed, multi-paragraph dream that I record and then completely forget days later. I'm so glad that I record them as soon as I wake, so I'm able to steward them well. I also believe our dreams can be wonderful places to spend our daily quiet times with the Lord. I will sometimes scroll back a few weeks or months and ask Holy Spirit which He wants to spend time on together and make that our conversation for the day. If these dreams are intimate communications from my Friend and Father, why wouldn't they be a wonderful way to connect with Him?"

Lee K.

"As one who has not been a prolific dreamer, I have appreciated that when I do have a dream I'd like to share and receive insight into; I know I have a trustworthy and willing dream community where I can be vulnerable and will be treated with respect.

"With one of my dreams, two or three people gave me prayerful input and it encouraged and confirmed my gifting and calling! They shared insights I had not thought of! They were as excited to see if what they interpreted resonated with me as I was to receive it!!"

Kevin P.

"Being in a community of dreamers and dream interpreters has been so incredibly rewarding. For many years, dreams were a bit of a mystery to me. They were fleeting, sometimes puzzling scenes that I'd barely remember in the morning. But studying about dreams through a Biblical lens has taught me that dreams are a new way for the Holy Spirit to speak to me. Having an intellectual framework for types of dreams, symbols and content has been a useful foundation in interpreting dreams, but I've learned that knowledge isn't the end game – it's a starting point inviting me to pursue a deeper relationship with the Lord and with others. By prayerfully seeking the Holy Spirit for clarity and discernment, I'm able to better understand what the Lord might be telling me through a dream. And by sharing dreams in a trusted, Godly community and practicing dream interpretation together, I've received new insights about my own dreams and been able to encourage others in interpreting their dreams. This community has been such a gift!"

Ashley W.

"The Lord delivered me from a dark oppression through a nightmare turned dream. Before meeting a fellow dreamer/dream community, I knew my dreams meant something, but I had no idea how to steward them or even pray through them. I didn't even know what to ask of God!

"Meeting my dream community changed my life. Literally. It's a mile marker in my life for learning prayer strategies, hearing the voice of God, discovering truth in the Word, as well as holding hands with fellow believers as they grow in these areas too. Seeing their eyes light up when it *clicks* is just as fun as when mine do!

"I've also made some of my best friends through my dream community. A deep sense of honoring one another is crucial for a thriving dream community. It's important to interact with humility, focusing on asking questions instead of speaking what you think.

"If you know no one to physically talk to about dreams, I suggest starting with a dreams course, either Kathy Gray or Steams Ministries &

John Paul Jackson's dream teachings! These are also great to do together as a group with your friends!"

Suzanna N.

"Being a part of a dream community has spurred me on to sharing with others about dream interpretation, especially with those who have never been exposed to it. It has also caused me personally to take my dreams more seriously, writing them down and dating them. I've learned to lean into them and ask the Lord questions, both about my dreams and other's dreams.

"My experience has been that consistently sharing our dreams with one another is vital to a thriving dream community. If you are not a part of a community that talks about dreams, I encourage you to find at least one friend you can talk 'dream interpretation' with. Encourage them to share with other friends, as you do as well and before you know it you may have a good group of dreamers!"

Catie T.

"I don't have many people in-person who are skilled at dream interpretations, so I rely pretty heavily on my long-distance community when I'm unsure about the meaning, and I ask Holy Spirit to make it clear. Sometimes dreams take months before I understand them, but once I do, it's been so encouraging to have people who 'get it' that I can call and tell! Telling someone about an encouraging dream, like if I receive some intel on how to pray or what to do next, feels like opening a gift surrounded by friends who say, 'Ooh I love that!'

"I test the waters in my 'real' community occasionally and ask people if they dream. When I share a dream with someone new to the idea, I usually just share interpretation instead of imagery.

"For example: 'God showed me in a dream that I needed to die to self and release my obsession with defending myself from slander.'

"I didn't say, 'In my dream someone's mouth turned into a machine gun, and they began accusing me with hundreds of bullets flying at me. I fell backwards into an empty grave and realized if I lay there, the bullets would pass over me, but if I sat up, I would get wounded. So, I lay there until they left.'"

REFLECTIONS

1. What are the potential benefits of collaborating with others in dream interpretation?

_____

_____

_____

2. Daniel sought the support of his friends to pray for understanding of the king's dream. Are there people in your circles you turn to for help in understanding dreams and visions?

_____

_____

_____

3. Have you ever experienced a moment when sharing a dream or vision with others led to greater clarity and insight? How did that process unfold?

_____

_____

_____

4. What practical steps can you take in being intentional about expanding your circle of influence to include people who value biblical dream interpretation?

_____

_____

_____

5. How can you help foster a safe, open environment for sharing dreams and challenges, and what qualities do you feel make a dream community effective?

_____

_____

_____

Chapter 19

CONCLUSION

Our incredible God is the Master Storyteller! Before time itself, He began to craft tales filled with awe-inspiring wonder, heart-pounding drama, fierce battles, stories of redemptive love, light-hearted humor, miraculous rescues, and glorious victories. Through the tapestry of history, He has woven His themes into the very fabric of the world.

Our Father, the great Author, has written a unique story for each of us, one that began long before we took our first breath. Is it any wonder that God would fashion stories, night parables, designed to draw us closer to Him - to partner with Him to achieve that beautiful destiny more fully for our lives, for our families, communities, and the nations? His invitation is to discover this story, both individually and collectively, as we journey during our time on earth.

In absorbing the content of these pages, even if you don't fully agree with every perspective, I hope that you have been stirred to embrace that dreaming and dream interpretation was God's idea from the beginning. Maybe even some of your own dreams have come into sharper focus as you've read. I pray that you grasp how the crucial role of dreams is demonstrated throughout the Word. In His great love the Father designed us to work with the Holy Spirit to steward dreams the way God intended - through a biblical lens. I hope this has drawn you to put your hand in the Father's hand and journey through the Scriptures together to form your own convictions about dreams and their interpretation.

There's a great need today for wise, Holy Spirit reliant, biblically grounded dream interpretation in our culture. Even if you consider yourself a non-dreamer, your ability to interpret dreams is still invaluable to the Body of Christ and to your communities. People all around us are hungry to know they are valued. Their ears itch to hear that they have a unique purpose designed by their Creator, that God knows their name, that the One who is Love is pursuing them! Helping someone understand their dreams is a powerful opportunity to reveal the Father's heart for them, whether they follow Jesus or not. Your help with their dream could be what God uses to turn them to Himself and bring them out of darkness into Light!

"Speak Lord, your servants are listening!"
~ 1 Samuel 3:10

Chapter 20

BLESSING AND IMPARTATION

May you discover the heart of the Father, the friendship of Jesus, and the power of the Holy Spirit through your dreams. May the Love of God saturate your body, soul, and spirit. May the Fear of the Lord and the water of the Word cleanse you and grant you Heaven's wisdom. May you dream more than ever before! May you remember your dream encounters and find joy in collaborating with God and others as you unravel their mysteries.

I declare protection over you and your household as you sleep, in the name of Jesus, according to Psalm 4:8 and Psalm 127:1, 2.[88] May the Holy Spirit uncover any hidden access the enemy uses to bring disturbance. May God grant you the grace and courage to remove that access and establish firm, protective boundaries. May you confidently say, *"The Lord is my refuge and fortress, my God in whom I trust!"*[89]

May you develop a deep love for dreaming and excel in your ability to interpret them with skill and understanding. May God give you the Spirit of wisdom and revelation, so that you would know Him more deeply. May the eyes of your heart be enlightened so that you will be filled with hope as you discover His unique calling for you.[90] May you grow to live in the love of the Father more fully than you ever thought possible.

May God breathe on all you yield to Him.

With love,
Kathy Gray

GLOSSARY OF DREAM ELEMENTS

COMMON DREAM SYMBOLS &
SUGGESTED MEANINGS

These symbols are a starting point for processing metaphorically rather than serving as a comprehensive dream element resource. The symbols and their meanings are not intended to be definitive or absolute, as the interpretation of a symbol can vary depending on the dream's context and the individual dreamer. While many of these symbols are found in scripture and carry clear, established meanings, their interpretation can still vary depending on the dream's context and the individual dreamer. Even with scriptural words or symbols, several meanings can apply.

As you reflect on your dream, invite the Holy Spirit to bring insight as you explore possible meanings. If your dream includes a particular symbol, consider conducting a Bible word search to gain deeper, scriptural insight.

ACTIONS

Being chased – Being pursued

(+) Pursued by God

(-) Threatened by enemy, enemy trying to cause fear

(Lamentations 4:19, Luke 15, Ezekiel 34:11, Psalm 23:6, Psalm 143:3)

Brushing Teeth

(+) Polishing / increasing understanding (*see teeth*)

Birthing / Labor

(+) Bringing forth something new that requires nurturing, intercession/prayer, new ministry/era, answered prayer, salvation

(Micah 4:10, 1 Kings 18:42, Revelation 12:5-6, 1 Samuel 1:20, John 3:3)

Chasing – Pursuing something

(+) Victory over enemies, righteousness

(-) Chasing physical wealth, pursuing evil

(Leviticus 26:7-8, 1 Timothy 6:11, Isaiah 1:23, Isaiah 59:7)

Cooking / Preparing Food

(+) Preparing spiritual nourishment, pastor, discipleship, hospitality, spiritual honor / nourishment in the midst of trouble

(John 21:17, Acts 2:46–47, Psalm 23)

Dying – *rarely literal*

(+) Something coming to an end – issue in their life / industry they represent / relationship, dying to self

(-) Spiritual death, end of a relationship

(1 Corinthians 6:14, Galatians 2:20, Luke 9:23, Jeremiah 9:21, Romans 6:23)

Eating – Feeding on spiritual food

(+) Feeding on godly things, fellowship, will of God

(-) Feeding on ungodly things

(Matthew 6:11, Jeremiah 15:16, Acts 2:46, John 4:34, Isaiah 44:20)

Falling

(+) Overcome by God's presence, in need of friends

(-) Feeling out of control, pushed by the enemy

(Acts 9:4, John 18:6, Ecclesiastes 4:9-12, Psalm 38:17, Psalm 118:13)

Fishing

(+) Evangelism

(-) Probing for information

(Matthew 4:19)

Fighting

(+) Spiritual battle, fight of faith, God fighting for us

(-) Relational conflict

(Ephesians 6:12, 1 Timothy 6:12, Exodus 14:14, James 4:1-2)

Flying

(+) Ability to rise above circumstances, result of waiting on the Lord, escape, higher perspective, ability to maneuver in the Spirit, in the Spirit

(Isaiah 40:30-31, Psalm 55:6, Acts 8:39)

Haircut

(+) Trimming what's unnecessary, pruning, cleansing from sin

(-) Loss of strength or anointing, wisdom cut short, period of consecration cut short

(John 15:1-2, Leviticus 14:8, Judges 16:19, Numbers 6:1-21) *(see hair)*

Hiding – Seeking protection

(+) Hiding in the Lord, hiding from danger

(-) Shame, deception, or insecurity

(Psalm 91, Psalm 32:7, Joshua 2:1-8, Genesis 3:8-10, Joshua 7:1-21, 1 Samuel 10:22)

Kiss

(+) Agreement, affection, the Lord's love for us, friendship

(-) betrayal, deception

(Song of Solomon 1:2, Psalm 85:10, Romans 16:16, Luke 22:47-48, Proverbs 27:6)

Losing purse, wallet, or money – Loss of identity or favor *(see purse/wallet)*

(Galatians 3:1-3)

Naked

(+) Vulnerable, innocence, transparent, nothing to hide

(-) Shame, exposed, unprepared

(Genesis 2:25, Hebrew 4:13, Genesis 3:7, 1 Thessalonians 2:3-5, Isaiah 47:3, Revelation 16:15)

Pregnancy

(+) Preparatory stage, reproducing, answered prayer, something new, expectancy

(Luke 1:24-25, Matthew 1:20, 1 Samuel 1:20, Isaiah 7:14)

Running

(+) Race of faith, refuge in the name of the Lord, obedience, avoiding temptation

(-) Disobedience, avoidance, cowardice, eager to do wrong

(1 Corinthians 9:24–26, Proverbs 18:10, Psalm 119:32, Jonah 1:3, Revelation 21:8, Proverbs 28:1, Proverbs 6:18)

Inability to Run

(-) Fear impeding your spiritual walk, spiritual hindrance

Singing

(+) Worship, deep love of God, spiritual weapon, freedom and deliverance

(-) Lament, sorrow, false worship, insincere worship

(Psalm 95:1–2, Zephaniah 3:17, 2 Chronicles 20:21–22, Acts 16:25–26, Psalm 137:1–4, Amos 6:4–5, Isaiah 29:13)

Sleeping

(+) Rest, physical death, God's intervention, faith in the storm

(-) Exposed, prayerlessness, laziness (spiritual and in the natural)

(Psalm 4:8, Psalm 127:2, John 11:11, 1 Thessalonians 4:13-14, Genesis 2:2, 1 Samuel 26:12, Mark 4:38 Revelation 16:15, Matthew 26:40-41, Proverbs 6:9-11)

Speech
Shouting / Yelling

(+) Celebration, war cry

(-) Feeling out of control, venting anger

(Psalm 98:4, 1 Samuel 4:5, Joshua 6:20, Proverbs 29:11, Proverbs 15:1)

Whisper

(+) Presence of God

(-) conspiring, gossip

(1 Kings 19:12, Psalm 41:7, Proverbs 18:8.)

Spying

(+) Prophetic, discerning of spirits, discerning enemy schemes

(-) Religious legalism, secret criticism

(2 Kings 6:8-12, 2 Corinthians 2:11, Luke 20:20, 2 Samuel 6:16)

Swimming

(+) Moving in things of the Spirit, immersed in the Spirit

(-) deep sorrow

(Ezekiel 47:5, Matthew 3:11, Psalm 6:6)

Taking a shower

(+) Spiritual cleansing, cleansing through the word of God, generational blessing

(1 John 1:9, Titus 3:5, John 15:3, Isaiah 44:3)

Taking a Test

(+) Time of testing: trust in God, reveal the heart, refining, test obedience, reveal identity, prove faith, increase strength, increase perseverance,

(Genesis 22:1, Deuteronomy 8:2, Psalm 66:10, Matthew 4:1, 1 Peter 1:6–7, James 1:2–4)

Teeth loose, crooked, falling out

(+) Invitation to ask for understanding

(-) Losing understanding, iniquity

(Proverbs 2:6, James 1:5, Psalm 119:34, Romans 1:21–22, Ephesians 4:18, Psalm 119:130, Psalm 51:2–3)

Using the toilet

(+) Cleansing process, inner healing, eliminate toxins; in public – cleansing process that will be visible to others

(Deuteronomy 23:12–14, 2 Corinthians 7:1, Psalm 51:1–4)

Waking up

(+) Spiritual alertness, awareness of prophetic revelation, new life

(Ephesians 5:14, Romans 13:11, Zechariah 4:1, Mark 5:41)

Walking

(+) Walk with God, ways of God, humility, walk by the Spirit, calling

(-) Spiritual darkness, fleshly, sin, deception

(Genesis 6:9, Deuteronomy 10:12, Micah 6:8, Galatians 5:16, Ephesians 4:1, 1 John 1:6-7, Jeremiah 7:24)

Washing hands

(+) Innocent of guilt, repentance, assistant to a leader/prophet

(-) External ritual

(Matthew 27:24, James 4:8, Mark 7:5–8, 2 Kings 3:11)

ANIMALS

Alligator

(-) Influencer who launches a verbal attack, powerful mouth, twists the truth, long powerful tail (tale), hidden

(Psalm 109:2-3, Psalm 140:1-3, Psalm 41:9, 1 Corinthians 5:11)

Ant

(+) Diligence, wisdom, small

(-) Nuisance

(Proverbs 6:6-8, 30:24-25)

Armadillo – Shell for protection from predators, unearth hidden things - great diggers, solitary by nature

Bear

(-) Predator, over-bearing, dangerous if confronted, powerful spiritual force, "bear robbed of her cubs" – anger, "bear market" – economic downturn, appears gentle but deadly, suddenly unreasonable, issues that "hibernate" and then surface again

(+) "Bear hug" - warm and affectionate *(Bear is rarely positive)*

(Proverbs 28:15, 2 Kings 2:23–25, Proverbs 17:12, Revelation 13:2, 2 Samuel 17:8)

Polar bear – Religious spirit, oppresses the flock (Matthew 23:1-35)

Bee

(+) Working in unity, produces honey - abundant resources, gracious words, healing balm, promised land, word of God

(-) Enemies swarming, painful attack

(Exodus 3:8, Proverbs 16:24, Psalm 119:103, Deuteronomy 1:44, Psalm 118:12)

Beast of the field, wild beasts

(+) Untamed creation

(-) Demonic forces

(Genesis 2:19, Mark 1:12-13, Isaiah 56:9)

Bird

(+) God's provision, trust

(-) enemy stealing God's word

(Matthew 6:33, Matthew 13:4)

Butterfly

(+) Transformation, new life, new creation, feeds on the Word (nectar)

(-) Flighty

(2 Corinthians 5:17, Psalm 19:10, Ephesians 4:14, 1 Kings 18:21)

Cat

(+) Land on their feet, doesn't follow the crowd

(-) Independent thinking, willful, cannot be herded, black cat — typically associated with witchcraft, the occult

(Psalm 37:23-24, 2 Corinthians 4:8–9, Romans 12:2, Proverbs 28:26, Romans 12:16, Isaiah 53:6)

Cattle/Cow

(+) Provision, wealth

(-) Cow – False protection, tradition above truth "sacred cow"

(Genesis 41:26, Genesis 13:2, Exodus 9:1-7, Mark 7:8–9, 13, Colossians 2:8)

Camel

(+) Wealth and provision, perseverance in desert, prophet or evangelist calling

(Isaiah 60:6, Matthew 3:4)

Chicken

(-) Fear, cowardice

Deer

(+) Sure footed, thirsty for God, healing, someone who is "dear"

(Psalm 18:33, Psalm 42:1, Is. 35:6)

Dog

(+) Friend (man's best friend)

(-) Growling dog – friend turned on you, betrayal, corrupt and lazy leaders

(Proverbs 18:24, Psalm 41:9, Matthew 26:14-16, Isaiah 56:10-11)

Donkey

(+) Humility, burden bearer

(-) Stubborn, lacking understanding

(Zechariah 9:9, Matthew 21:5, Proverbs 26:3, Genesis 16:12, Psalm 32:9)

Duck

(+) "Water off duck's back" – rise above offense, "to duck" to avoid something

(-) "Sitting duck" – vulnerable to attack

(Proverbs 12:16, 1 Peter 3:9, Ecclesiastes 7:21, Proverbs 27:12)

Eagle

(+) God's protection and nurture, culturally used to symbolize the prophetic gift

(-) Overconfident pride and arrogance

(Deuteronomy 32:11-12, Exodus 19:4, Obadiah 1:4)

Elephant

(+) Big issue, great impact, long memory

Fish

(+) People (fishers of men), miraculous sign, provision

(-) Disobedience, oppressed vulnerable people

(Matthew 4:19; Luke 5:6, John 21:11; Luke 9:16, Mark 6:41-43, Jonah 1:17, Habakkuk 1:14–17)

Flies

(-) Presence of garbage / dead things, false god of creation

(Exodus 8:20-32)

Frogs

(-) Unclean spirit, false god of fertility

(Revelation 16:13, Exodus 8:1-15)

Goat

(+) Atonement, provision

(-) unrighteous, scapegoat, sin that needs to be dealt with, demon god

(Leviticus 16, Proverbs 27:27, Matthew 25:31–46, Leviticus 17:7)

Hornet

(+) Terror from God to drive out enemies, supernatural help in obtaining God's destiny

(Exodus 23:28; Deut. 7:20)

Horse

(+) Strength, power, authority, justice for oppressed (mighty steed in battle)

(-) Not trusting God; trust in earthly strength

(Psalm 33:17, Revelation19:11, Zech. 10:3, Isaiah 31:1, Psalm 147:10, Psalm 20:7)

Lamb

(+) Jesus Christ, sacrifice / offering, children, believers, young believers, innocence

(1 Peter 1:18-19, Revelation 5:6, John 1:29, Isaiah 53:7, Isaiah 40:11, Exodus 12:21)

Lion

(+) Authority, Jesus Christ, boldness, the righteous, moral courage, power

(-) Enemy, adversary, devourer, destruction, divine discipline, predator

(Proverbs 20:2, Proverbs 28:1, Revelation 5:5, 1 Peter 5:8, Jeremiah 4:7)

Lizard

(+) Resourcefulness, regeneration, adaptability

(-) Unclean, impurity

(Proverbs 30:28, Leviticus 11:30)

Locusts

(+) Call to repentance, restoration, prophetic lifestyle

(-) Divine devastation, devourers, call to armies

(Joel 2:12–14, Joel 2:25, Matthew 3:4, Joel 1:4, Exodus 10:12–15)

Manta ray

(+) Person who moves smoothly/glides/flies in the spirit, not stinging (gentle), non-aggressive, meekness - gentle giants

(Romans 8:14, 1 Corinthians 2:10-13, Galatians 5:23, Matthew 5:5, Numbers 12:3)

Monkey

(-) Mischief, foolish behavior, addiction (monkey on my back)

Mule

(+) Humility, peaceful reign, strength burden bearer

(-) Stubborn, sterile (half horse, half donkey), stubborn, lack of understanding

(1 Kings 1:33, Mark 11:2, Psalm 32:9)

Octopus – *Represents a spirit / person*

(-) Control and manipulation (many arms), deception (Camouflage), deep dark things (occult), clouds the situation (black ink), entanglement in sin, often associated with Jezebel

(Micah 2:1, Proverbs 26:24–26, 2 Peter 2:20, Psalm 64:5–6, Ephesians 4:14, Ephesians 5:11, Revelation 2:20–22)

Otter

(+) Joy in creation, playful, childlike, delights in operating in the Spirit

(Ecclesiastes 3:12–13, Matthew 18:3, Proverbs 17:22, Romans 14:17)

Rat

(-) Moral / spiritual defilement, disease, divine judgment, spiritual decay (feeds on garbage), teller of secrets / betrayal

(Isaiah 66:17, Leviticus 11, 1 Samuel 6, Proverbs 11:13, Luke 22:48)

Rooster

(+) Wake-up call, conviction, restoration

(Matthew 26:34, John 21:15–19)

Scorpion

(-) Stinging words; demonic power; torment; betrayal / harmful intent

(Ezekiel 2:6; Luke 10:19; Revelation 9:3-5; Luke 11:12)

Sharks

(-) Powerful predator, aggression, ruthless ambition, hidden, eats little fish, spiritual predator

(Ezekiel 34, Psalm 55:21, Jeremiah 23:1, Philippians 3:19, 2 Peter 2:1–3)

Sheep

(+) People, believers, the lost, the church, wealth

(-) Leaderless, helpless, sin, wandering from God, oppression

(Psalm 100:3; John 21:17; Isaiah 53:6, Matthew 18:12-14; 1 Peter 5:2, Job 1:3, Matthew 9:36, Numbers 27:17, Isaiah 53:6, Zechariah 11:4–7)

Snakes – Rarely positive

(+) Shrewd, wise, healing (serpent lifted up on a tree)

(-) Lie - long tails (tales) with a mouth, deceiver, cunning, judgment

(Matthew 10:16, Numbers 21:8–9; John 3:14–15, Revelation 12:9, Genesis 3:1, John 8:44)

Venomous – Lies and accusations have paralyzing effect, nerves, are painful

Python – Lies that constrict, squeeze the life out of its prey, restrict breath (Holy Spirit)

Spider

(-) Witchcraft, rebellion, occultic, web of deception, entrapment, must be destroyed

(1 Samuel 15:23, Ephesians 5:11, Acts 19:18–19, Micah 5:12, Nahum 3:4, Galatians 3:1)

Squirrel

(+) Industrious, preparation, alert

(-) Flighty, squirrely, indecision

(Proverbs 6:6–8, Proverbs 10:4, Ephesians 6:18, James 1:6–8, 1 Kings 18:21)

Swine / Pig

(-) Unclean, impurity, demonic, reject / trample / attack truth tellers, moral degradation, returning to sin

(Leviticus 11:7–8, Deuteronomy 14:8, Mark 5:11–13, Matthew 7:6, Luke 15:15–16, 2 Peter 2:22)

Tiger

(-) Predator, known for its colors, orange (stubbornness) and black (soulish issues); a soulish problem that's difficult to overcome, a stronghold

(Jeremiah 7:24, Romans 2:5, Exodus 32:9, Isaiah 30:1, 2 Corinthians 10:3-5)

Turtle

(+) Steady progress, slow change, guarding heart, long life

(-) Self-protective, Snapping – self-protective person who lashes out, hiding, fear of man

(Hebrews 10:36, Proverbs 4:23, Psalm 90:12, 1 Samuel 10:22, Proverbs 29:25, Isaiah 51:12)

Whales

(+) Someone with large influence, deep in spirit, they migrate, international ministry, cross borders

(-) Large issue

(1 Corinthians 2:10-16, Acts – Paul's missionary journeys)

Wolves

(-) Mislead believers, enemies of God's people, corrupt leaders in the church, oppressive rulers

(Matthew 7:15, Matthew 10:16, Acts 20:29–30, Ezekiel 22:27)

BODY PARTS

Arm

(+) Strength, faith, salvation, redemption, protection, embrace

(-) Trust in human strength, oppression / abuse of power

(Psalm 18:34, Isaiah 52:10, Exodus 6:6, Isaiah 40:11, Jeremiah 17:5, Psalm 10:15, Ezekiel 30:22)

Back

(+) Past, remembrance, rearguard, burden bearing, daily surrender, repentance

(-) Past, rebellion, back-biting, burdens, vulnerable to attack, betrayal

(Psalm 77:11–12, Exodus 14:19–20, Galatians 6:2, Luke 9:23, Galatians 5:15, Jeremiah 2:27, Matthew 26:14-16)

Beard

(+) Maturity, dignity, unity

(-) Suffering – plucked out

(2 Samuel 10:4–5, Psalm 133:1–2, Isaiah 50:6)

Blood

(+) Life, redemption, forgiveness of sin, cleansing and purity, covenant

(-) Bloodshed, guilt, defiled land, child sacrifice / abortion

(Leviticus 17:14, Ephesians 1:7, 1 John 1:7-9, Matthew 26:28, Genesis 4:10, Isaiah 59:3, Numbers 35:33, Psalm 106:37–38)

Ear

(+) Listening with intent to obey, hearing that gives life, the Lord hearing our prayers

(-) Hardened heart

(Matthew 11:15, Isaiah 55:3, Psalm 34:15, Matthew 13:15, Zechariah 7:11)

Earlobe – Consecration, cleansing (Leviticus 8:23-24, Leviticus 14:14)

Elbow – Ability to hold, embrace

Eyes – Vision, heart perception, light to the inner man, seeing in the spirit realm, being watched

(-) Spiritual blindness, lust, proud heart, seduction

(Ephesians 1:18, 2 Kings 6:17, Psalm 101:3, Matthew 13:15, 1 John 2:16, Proverbs 21:4, Proverbs 6:25)

Face

(+) Presence, favor, determination, person's identity, reflects the heart - cheerful heart, shining – God's glory, Jesus' face – God's glory, wisdom

(-) Hidden - afraid of God, distance, reflects the heart – fallen

(Psalm 27:8, Numbers 6:24–26, Isaiah 50:7, Proverbs 15:13, 2 Corinthians 3:7, Ecclesiastes 8:1, 2 Corinthians 4:6, Exod. 3:6, Psalm 13:1, Genesis 4:5–6)

Faceless

(+) Supernatural being, angel, the Lord *(Ask questions about the characteristics of this being.)*

Fingers – Power and authority, five-fold gifts, works of God

(-) Accusation and blame, hypocrisy lack of compassion

(Exodus 8:19, Isaiah 58:9, Exodus 31:18, Matthew 23:4)

Feet – Walk in life

(+) Carry the gospel, acts of service, worship, holy ground, learning

(-) Deformed - not walking in calling

(John 13:5, Isaiah 52:7, Luke 7:38, Joshua 5:15, Luke 10:39, John 12:3)

Hair

(+) Strength, covering, consecrated to God, anointing, gray hair – wisdom/ maturity, glory

(-) vanity *(Note color if different than in the natural)*

(Judges 16:17, Numbers 6:5, 1 Corinthians 11:15, Proverbs 16:31, 1 Timothy 2:9)

Hands

(+) Authority, power, ownership, blessing, worship, friendship, work

(-) Evil, bloodshed

(Isaiah 48:13, Psalm 95:4-5, Mark 10:16, Psalm 90:17, Psalm 63:4, Psalm 90:17, 1 Thessalonians 4:11-12 Isaiah 1:15)

Head

(+) Source, Jesus, blessing

(-) Crushed – total defeat, shaking head / disapproval

(1 Corinthians 11:3, Ephesians 5:23, Exodus 18:25, Proverbs 10:6, Gen. 3:15, Psalm 109:25)

Heart

(+) Source of affections, devotion, words (+ or -), life, true self, follows what we value

(-) Hardened – pride, stubbornness, resistant to God's will, unbelief

(Proverbs 4:23, Matthew 12:34, Deuteronomy 6:5, Matthew 6:21, Daniel 5:20, Hebrews 3:7-8, Mark 8:17)

Heel

(+) Victory over the enemy

(-) Betrayal, person is "a heel" – dishonorable / selfish, pursuit – on my heels, cunning / grasping

(Genesis 3:15, Psalm 41:9, John 13:18, Gensis 25:26)

Knees

(+) Prayer, submission, generational blessing

(-) Feeble – tiredness, fear

(Luke 22:41, Philippians 2:10–11, Genesis 50:23, Isaiah 35:3–4, Hebrews 12:12)

Lips – Speech

(+) Praise, prayer, blessing, reveals the heart

(-) Lying lips, reveals the heart, double standard, cursing, seduction

(Psalm 34:1, Proverbs 12:22, Luke 6:45, James 3:9-10, Proverbs 5:3–4)

Nakedness

(+) Transparency, humility, no guile, exposed

(-) Shame, exposed

(Genesis 2:25, Job 1:21, Genesis 3:7, Hebrews 4:13)

Neck – Decision making, determines where the head turns

(+) Beauty and strength

(-) Stubborn, pride, subjection

(Song of Solomon 4:4, Isaiah 3:16-17, Exodus 32:9, Joshua 10:24)

Nose

(+) Discernment "knows," accuracy "right on the nose," spiritual sensitivity, pleasing sacrifice, able to smell something out

(-) Strife, judgment of God – hook in nose

(Psalm 115:6, 8, Proverbs 30:33, Isaiah 37:29, Ephesians 5:2)

Shoulder – Government, strength, burden bearing, holy responsibilities, authority

(-) burdens, oppression, rebellion, stubbornness

(Isaiah 9:6, Psalm 81:6, Zechariah 7:11, Numbers 7:9, Isaiah 22:22)

Side

(+) Relationship, equality and companionship, relationship restored, birth of church through water and blood

(-) Vulnerability to attack, relational wounding

(Genesis 2:21-24, John 19:34)

Right – What you have faith to do, power, ability

Left – What you are born to do

Stomach (Belly / Womb)

(+) and (-): heart, desire, appetite, center of emotions, innermost parts, spiritual source of life, physical stomach / abdomen

(Philippians 3:19, Song of Solomon 5:4, John 7:38, 1 Timothy 5:23)

Teeth

(+) Understanding

(-) Falling out - loss of ability to understand

Eye teeth – seeing with understanding

Wisdom teeth – wisdom

Thigh

(+) Oath, covenant, faith, humbling

(-) Judgment

(Genesis 24:2–3, Psalm 45:3, Genesis 32:25, Numbers 5:21–27, Revelation 19:16)

Toes

    (+) Balance, consecration to walk in God's ways

    (-) Defeat and judgment, instability in world powers

    (Leviticus 8:23–24, Judges 1:6–7, Daniel 2:41–43)

CLOTHING

Belt

(+) Truth, strength, readiness

(-) God's people defiled - useless when corrupted by leaving God to follow the world

(Ephesians 6:14, Psalm 93:1, Luke 12:35 KJV, Jeremiah 13:1-11)

Clothing that doesn't fit – Walking in something I'm not called to or haven't grown into yet.

(1 Samuel 17:38-39)

Coat / Robe / Mantle

(+) Righteousness, royalty, honor, authority, identity (note type of coat worn)

(-) Mockery, suffering (Jesus stripped of His robe)

(Isaiah 61:10, Revelation 7:13–14, Esther 6:7-8, Genesis 37:3, Genesis 41:42, Matthew 27:28–29, 1 Kings 19:19)

Pants – Spiritual covering for walk, in charge ("wears the pants"), ready for assignment, thirsty for God

(Isaiah 61:10, 1 Peter 1:13, Psalm 42:1)

Shoes – Peace, gospel, readiness, covenant, ownership, preparation for function/purpose *(note type and color)*

(-) Shame/disgrace for shirking responsibility

Missing shoes – Lack of peace, protection

Shoes off – Holy ground

(Ephesians 6:15, Exodus 3:5, Ruth 4:7, Deuteronomy 25:9–10)

Shorts

Exposure, leisure, partial covering, something cut off, partial fulfillment

Socks

(+) Comfort, at ease

(-) Not sturdy or supportive, slippery, appear to be a covering but not sufficient, not made for action

Swimwear – Ability to maneuver in the Spirit, ready for things of the Spirit

Underwear – Intimacy, exposure of private issues

Wedding Dress – Bride of Christ, righteous deeds of believers (Ephesians 5:25–27, Revelation 19:7–8)

Wool

(+) Purity, sinlessness

(Isaiah 1:18)

FOOD

Bread

(+) Jesus, Jesus' body, the Word of God, basic provision, literal/symbolic daily sustenance, miraculous provision, fellowship, hidden influence (leaven)

(-) Idleness, sorrow, hardship, sin / lies, hypocrisy (leaven)

(John 6:35, Matthew 4:3–4, Genesis 3:19, Exodus 16:4, Acts 2:46, Proverbs 31:27, Psalm 127:2, Deuteronomy 16:3, Proverbs 20:17, Luke 12:1)

Cheese – Important person (big cheese), over the top (cheesy), fake, artificial

Eggs

(+) Fertility, new beginnings, new life, basic sustenance, good gifts, yolk – anointing that breaks the yoke, promise yet to be fulfilled (hatched)

(-) Oppression (yoke), fragile, easily broken

(Exodus 23:25–26, John 15:4-6, 2 Corinthians 5:17, Luke 11:11–12, Isaiah 10:27)

Honey

(+) Word of God, pleasant words, healing balm, internalizing God's message

(-) Seduction, overindulgence

(Psalm 119:103, Proverbs 16:24, Ezekiel 27:17, Ezekiel 3:3, Proverbs 5:3–4, Proverbs 25:27)

Fruit

(+) Evidence of the Spirit, blessing and provision, abiding in Christ, changed life

(-) Bad character

(Galatians 5:22-23, Genesis 1:29, John 15:5,8, Matthew 7:17–20, Matthew 3:8)

Meat

(+) Solid spiritual food, provision

(-) Stumbling block, craving, judgment

(Hebrews 5:12–14, 1 Corinthians 8:1–13, Exodus 16:11–13)

Milk

(+) Spiritual hunger, provision, promise

(-) Spiritual immaturity

(1 Peter 2:2, Exodus 3:8, 1 Corinthians 3:1–2)

Olives / Olive oil

(+) Anointing, healing, provision and blessing, gladness

(-) Crushed, suffering – Gethsemane means "olive press"

(Exodus 30:22–25, James 5:14, Deuteronomy 8:8, Isaiah 61:3, Matthew 26:36-46)

Wine

(+) Joy, celebration, fellowship, blood of Jesus, new covenant, prosperity, restoration, transforming miracle

(-) Drunkenness, judgment

(Psalm 104:15, Ecclesiastes 9:7, Exodus 29:40, Luke 22:20, Amos 9:13, Proverbs 20:1, Ephesians 5:18, John 2:1-11, Jeremiah 25:15, Revelation 14:10)

MODES OF TRANSPORTATION

Airplane – Ability to go higher in the Spirit, ministry / church, dependence on Holy Spirit, carried to your destiny *(Note type/ function and color of vehicle)*

Bicycle

(+) Humble journey, forward motion

(-) Self-effort, without power of Holy Spirit

(1 Peter 5:6, Zechariah 4:6, 2 Timothy 3:5, 1 Corinthians 2:4, Galatians 3:3)

Bus

(+) Groups with a common destination, large ministry, church, led by the Spirit (driver)

(-) Missed opportunities

(Acts 2:46, John 16:13, Exodus 13:21–22, Psalm 106:24, Joel 2:25)

Boat

(+) Journey in the Spirit, ministry, salvation, sailboat (powered by spirit), speed boat

(-) Lacks depth (skims the surface)

(Luke 5:3, 1 Peter 3:20, John 3:8, James 1:23-24) *(See water)*

Car

(+) Individual ministry / vocation / destiny, Spirit-empowered

(Psalm 32:8, Zechariah 4:6)

Convertible

(+) Open heaven

Motorcycle

(+) Ability to maneuver, season of operating individually, powerful individual ministry

(-) Separated, lone ranger

(Matthew 3:1–3, 1 Kings 18:22, Proverbs 18:1, 1 Corinthians 12:14-18)

Plane

(+) Group operating at high level in the Spirit, powerful ministry, prophetic ministry (carried by the Spirit), high perspective (Isaiah 40:31-32, John 3:8)

Submarine

(+) Searches the deep things, stealth in the spirit (Romans 11:33, 1 Corinthians 2:10, 2 Kings 6:8-12)

Trains

(+) Move of God (many groups going the same direction), denomination, corporation

(-) On the wrong track, runaway train

(Colossians 1:5–6, Acts 5:12–14, Philippians 2:1–2, Jeremiah 6:16–17, Proverbs 14:12)

Truck

(+) Gift of service, endures over the long haul (semi-truck), supplies, burden bearer

(Romans 12:6–7, 1 Peter 4:10–11, Galatians 6:2)

NATURE

Cliff

(+) Refuge, God's protection

(-) Arrogance/untouchable, treachery, contempt due to familiarity

(Psalm 61:2, 2 Samuel 22:2-3, Obadiah 1:3, Luke 4:29)

Cloud

(+) God's Presence, God's glory, God's protection and covering, prophetic promise

(-) Judgment

(Exodus 13:21-22, Exodus 24:16-18, Revelation 1:7, Psalm 91:4, 1 Kings 18:44)

Desert

(+) Time of testing, spiritual restoration, place of transformation, humbling process, learning dependence, spiritual dryness, seeking God, supernatural provision, repentance

(-) Consequence for disobedience

(Matthew 4:1-2, Hosea 2:14-15, Isaiah 35:1-2, Psalm 63:1, Exodus 17:6, Matthew 3:3, Numbers 14:33-34)

Earthquake

(+) God's power and Presence, deliverance, the voice of the Lord, shaking

(-) Judgment for evil and oppression, God acting on the prayers of the saints

(Exodus 19:18, Matthew 27:51, Acts 16:25-26, Psalm 29:5, Haggai 2:6-7, Joshua 6:20, Revelation 8:4-5)

Field

(+) Harvest, the world, area of study / occupation, athletic competition, provision, condition of the heart

(-) Devastation because of sins of shepherds

(John 4:35, Mark 13:38, Ruth 2:2-3, Luke 8:5-8, Jeremiah 12:10)

Fire

(+) God's Presence and glory, Holy Spirit, empowerment, God's holiness, jealous God, refining to strengthen faith, ceaseless worship, the voice of the Lord

(-) Judgment for oppression and sin, eternal punishment

(Exodus 3:2, Exodus 13:21, Acts 2:3, Matthew 3:11, Deuteronomy 4:24, Malachi 3:2–3, 1 Peter 1:7, Psalm 29:7, Leviticus 6:12–13, Genesis 18:20, 19:24, Matthew 13:42)

Flowers

(+) Favor, beauty, intimacy, brevity of life, daily provision (don't worry), renewal / restoration, worship, fragrance of Christ

(-) Fear of aging, brevity of life

(Song of Solomon 1:14, Isaiah 40:6–8, Matthew 6:28–29, Isaiah 35:1–2, Ecclesiastes 12:5, 1 Kings 6:29-35, 2 Corinthians 2:15)

Garden

(+) Creation, intimacy with God, surrender, resurrection, prosperity, health, resurrection

(-) Suffering, loneliness, betrayal, death

(Genesis 2:8-9, Matthew 26:36, Isaiah 58:11, John 19:41–42, 1 Kings 4:25, Luke 22:39-48, John 19:41–42; 20:1–18)

Lightning

(+) God's holy Presence, power of the Word of God, God's throne, sovereign over creation, divine weapon

(-) Judgment of God, God acting on the prayers of the saints

(Exodus 19:16, Revelation 4:5, Job 37:3, 2 Samuel 22:15, Psalm 144:6, Revelation 8:4-5)

Moon

(+) Seasons / days / years, God's enduring covenant, beauty, mother, feasts/worship

(-) Idolatry, judgment of wicked rulers

(Genesis 1:16, Psalm 104:19, Psalm 89:37, Song of Solomon 6:10, Genesis 37:9, Psalm 81:3, Deuteronomy 4:19, Isaiah 13:10)

Mountain

(+) God's Kingdom, God's rule and authority, governing systems, spheres of influence

(-) Obstacles, evil governing in spheres of influence

(Isaiah 2:2–3, Daniel 2:35, 44, Jeremiah 51:25, Revelation 17:9, Mark 11:23)

Rock

(+) The Lord, (stability, faithfulness, immovable), Jesus, foundation for the wise, stability in the storm, Ekklesia, miraculous provision

(-) Hard place, offense to unbelievers, false source of strength, hard heart

(Psalm 18:2, 1 Corinthians 10:4, Matthew 7:24–25, Matthew 16:18, Exodus 17:6, Romans 9:32–33, Deuteronomy 32:31, Zechariah 7:12)

Sand

(+) Believers, abundance, innumerable, multiplication, God's thoughts towards us, time (sands of time)

(-) Weak foundation

(Genesis 22:17, Genesis 41:49, Psalm 139:17–18, Matthew 7:26)

Snow

(+) Righteousness, purity, forgiveness, holiness, favor and refreshing

(-) Harsh conditions

(Isaiah 1:18, Psalm 51:7, Daniel 7:9, Proverbs 25:13, Proverbs 31:21)

Stars

(+) Glory of God, believers, legacy, angels

(-) Fallen angels

(Psalm 19:1, Genesis 15:5, Job 38:7, Revelation 12:4, Isaiah 14:12)

Storm

(+) Trouble sent from God along with rescue, test, pressure for oppressors to turn to God, God bringing chaos for divine purpose, refuge from storm

(-) Treachery / oppression, attack, chaos, adversity

(Note: if light, storm is from the Lord)

(Psalm 107:23-28, Psalm 83:15-16, Mark 4:37-40, Psalm 55:8, Matthew 7:24–27)

Sun

(+) Glory of God, Father, the Lord's blessing, Jesus, times and seasons, end of a matter, new beginning

(-) Sin exposed

(Psalm 19:1–4, Genesis 37:9-10, Psalm 84:11, Malachi 4:2, Psalm 104:19, Exodus 17:12, Matthew 28:1, John 3:20-21)

Thunder

(+) God's holy Presence, power of the Word of God, the voice of the Lord, Father's voice misunderstood, God acting on the prayers of the saints

(-) Judgment on oppressors

(Exodus 19:16, John 12:28–29, Psalm 29:3, Revelation 8:4,5)

Tornado – Destructive storm: from God to destroy the wicked *(can be good - note the color)*, precedes heavenly encounter

(-) Death *(dark storm)*

(Jeremiah 30:23; Proverbs 10:25, Isaiah 40:23-24, 2 Kings 2:1, 11)

Tree

(+) Leader, lover of the Word, believers healed and restored, wisdom, life, delivered / healed by choosing life, healing of nations

(-) Knowledge of good and evil

(Daniel 4:22, Psalm 1:3, Isaiah 61:3, Proverbs 3:18, Genesis 2:9, Revelation 22:2)

Fig Tree

(+) Blessing / security / abundance, destiny and purpose, God's patience for us to repent, people

(-) Human effort to cover sin, fruitless life, hypocrisy, suffering and spiritual attack from failing to recognize God's authority and care

(Micah 4:4; 1 Kings 4:25, Psalm 1:3, Luke 13:6–9, Genesis 3:7, Matthew 21:18–19, Hosea 2:12)

Olive Tree

(+) Peace, hope, reconciliation, God's people, thriving, gentiles grafted in, two servants

(-) Consumed and broken because of idolatry

(Genesis 8:11, Romans 11:17, Psalm 52:8, Zechariah 4:3, 11–14, Revelation 11:4, Jeremiah 11:16)

Evergreen Tree

(+) Longevity, eternity, covenant, Everlasting God

(Genesis 21:33)

Valley

(+) Comforting Presence of God, door of hope, new beginnings, meek exalted, decision

(-) Sadness, discouragement

(Psalm 23:4, Hosea 2:15, Psalm 84:6, Isaiah 40:4, Joel 3:14, Psalm 84:6)

Water – Large body of water = influence; Smaller bodies of water = Holy Spirit

Ocean

(+) God as Master over chaos, baptism, works of the Lord, deliverance from distress, testing, many people, the nations, forgiveness, deep mysteries of God, displays glory of God

(-) The wicked, nations

(Matthew 8:27, 1 Corinthians 10:1-2, Psalm 107:23–30, Revelation 17:15, Micah 7:19, Isaiah 57:20)

Pond

(+) Small gathering of believers, small church, evangelism (fishing)

(-) stagnant church - no fresh flow of Holy Spirit

(Matthew 4:19, Jeremiah 2:13, Ezekiel 47:11)

Rain

(+) Blessing for obedience, favor, fruitfulness, blessing on our labors, revival, refreshing, God's Spirit, God's word, spiritual planting and harvest, teaching

(-) rain withheld - God's discipline, time of testing, storms of life

(Deuteronomy 28:12, Hosea 6:3, Leviticus 26:3-4, Isaiah 55:10–11, James 5:18, Joel 2:23, Deuteronomy 32:2, Amos 4:7–8, Matthew 7:24–27)

River

(+) Indwelling Holy Spirit, move of God, supernatural life, Word of God, baptism / cleansing / new life, promises of God – crossing over

(-) judgment for idolatry

(John 7 :38-39, Ezekiel 47:1-12, Ephesians 5:26, Deuteronomy 27:3, Matthew 3:13, 2 Kings 5, Isaiah 19:5-8)

Swimming Pool / Lake

(+) Local community of believers, exercising gifts of the Spirit, joy in the Holy Spirit, healing, cleansing

(John 5:2, 1 Corinthians 12:7, Hebrews 10:22)

Wind – *breath "ruach"*

(+) Holy Spirit, the voice of the Lord, creative power, revival, life

(-) Adversity, false teaching

(John 3:8, Psalm 29:8, Genesis 1:2, Ezekiel 37:9, Matthew 7:24–27, Matthew 8:26, Ephesians 4:14)

OBJECTS

Basket

(+) Offering the first fruit of income, supernatural provision/ multiplication, rescue

(-) Wickedness, lack of provision due to disobedience

(Deuteronomy 26:2, Mark 6:43, Acts 9:25, Exodus 2:3, Zechariah 5:11, Deuteronomy 28:17)

Bed

(+) Intimacy, longing, sexual purity and faithfulness, healing, dreams, thoughts, meditation, heart

(-) Spiritual adultery, agreement with evil, promiscuity, lust, sickness, laziness

(Song of Solomon 3:1, Hebrews 13:4, John 5:8, Daniel 2:29, Psalm 4:4, Hosea 7:14 - Isaiah 57:7–8, Hosea 4:14, Revelation 2:22, Proverbs 26:14)

Books

(+) Eternal life, God's commandments, covenant, judgment for the deeds of believers, record of those who fear the Lord / meditate on the Lord, the righteous, rule follower - going by the book

(-) The Law - "throw the book at," wicked removed, hard truths

(Revelation 20:12, 15, Joshua 1:8, Malachi 3:16, Exodus 24:7, Psalm 69:28, Ezekiel 3:3)

Cell phone / Computer

(+) Communication - with God and others, spiritual hearing, identity, connection, stored knowledge, connection, remembrance, vision, productivity

(-) Negative communication, unclean images/shows

(Matthew 11:15, Psalm 4:1, Deuteronomy 8:18, Psalm 77:11-12, Psalm 103:2, Proverbs 18:8, Exodus 23:1, Psalm 101:3)

Couch

(+) Rest / sabbath, leisure, family time

(-) Laziness, complacency and neglect – of duties and towards others, isolating, strategic phrasing - "couching words"

(Exodus 20:8–10, 1 Timothy 6:17, Deuteronomy 6:6-7, Proverbs 16:24, Amos 6:4, Hebrews 10:24-25, Proverbs 21:13)

Crown

(+) Honor & authority, life, righteousness, eternal reward, God's people on display

(-) Suffering, temporary earthly rewards, arrogant leaders

(Isaiah 61:3, James 1:12, 2 Timothy 4:8, Isaiah 62:3 John 19:2, 1 Corinthians 9:25, Isaiah 28:1)

Cup – *What we must experience - "drink"*

(+) The Lord, submission, justice on enemies

(-) Judgment, betrayal, pain, painful trials / discipline

(Psalm 16:5, Luke 22:42, Psalm 75:8, Mark 10:38, Isa. 51:17)

Horns

(+) Altar, salvation, Jesus Christ, strength, anointing

(-) Oppressive world powers, human pride

(Psalm 18:2, Luke 1:68–69, 1 Samuel 16:1, 13, Daniel 7:7–8, Psalm 75:4–5)

Key

(+) Open doors, spiritual authority, ability to open and shut doors, access to Kingdom of Heaven, access to hidden things, power over death, the solution - "key" to a problem

(-) Closed doors, gatekeeping, abuse of spiritual authority

(Isaiah 22:22, Matthew 16:19, Revelation 1:18, Luke 11:52)

Metal

Gold

(+) Glory of God, holiness, purity, royalty, wisdom

(-) Idolatry, sexual immorality

(Exodus 25, Matthew 2:11, Proverbs 3:13–14, Proverbs 21:3, Proverbs 25:11, Exodus 32:1–4, Revelation 17:4)

Silver

(+) Redemption, righteous words, refining

(-) Betrayal, slavery, moral corruption

(Exodus 30:12, Proverbs 10:20, Malachi 3:3, Matthew 26:14-15, Genesis 37:28, Isaiah 1:22)

Bronze

(+) God's righteous judgment, atonement, washing with water of the Word, cleansing from guilty conscience, healing

(-) Brazen, judgment for sin

(Exodus 40:6, Ephesians 5:25-27, Hebrews 10:22, Numbers 21:9, Isaiah 48:4)

Iron

(+) Friendship, spiritual accountability, God's absolute authority

(-) Slavery, spiritual bondage, obstinance

(Proverbs 27:17, Psalm 2:9, Deuteronomy 4:20, Psalm 107:10, Isaiah 48:4)

Money

(+) Provision, blessing, gaining favor, stewardship

(-) Greed, avarice (extreme greed for wealth) is root of evil, loss of favor, betrayal, self-reliance, bribe

(Proverbs 10:22, Matthew 25:14-30, 1 Timothy 6:10, Mark 14:11, Deuteronomy 8:13–14, Exodus 23:8)

Ring

(+) Authority, covenant, belonging

(-) Vanity, pride

(Genesis 41:42, Luke 15:22, Isaiah 3:16–23)

Pen

(+) Tongue, vision, word of God written on the heart

(-) Sin written on the heart

(Habakkuk 2:2, Psalm 45:1, Proverbs 3:3, Jeremiah 17:1)

Purse / Wallet

(+) Identity, favor, heart

(-) Lost purse - searching for identity

(Romans 8:16, Galatians 3:29, Colossians 2:6–7, Matthew 6:21)

Staff

(+) Power, authority, support, protection

(Exodus 14:16, Psalm 23:4, 1 Samuel 17:34-36)

Table

(+) Fellowship, provision, Presence of God, communion, hospitality

(-) Setting something aside/delay – "table it"

(Psalm 23:5, Exodus 25:30, 1 Corinthians 10:21, Luke 5:29, Acts 2:46–47)

Television

(+) Revelation "tell-a-vision," prophecy, media, far reaching influence

(-) Distraction, programming of the mind

(Ephesians 1:18, Psalm 101:3)

Toolbox

(+) Spiritual set of skills, resources, or tools

(2 Peter 1:5-8)

PEOPLE

Baby

(+) New believer, new ministry or responsibility, spiritual dependence

(-) Evil desires - sin

(1 Peter 2:2, 1 Corinthians 14:20, James 1:14-15)

Celebrities – Name meaning, characters they play, actions in the dream, influencers

Child

(+) Believer, blessing from God, humble, teachable, great in the Kingdom, celebrates the miraculous

(-) Immature

(Matthew 18:1–4, Psalm 127:3, Mark 10:14, Matthew 21:14-16, 1 Corinthians 13:11)

Clown

(-) Deceiver, exaggerated features, erratic behavior, hiding true feelings

(Proverbs 26:18–19, Proverbs 25:28)

Deceased Relative – Past issues, blessing or inheritance, healing or closure, calling passed on to you, message from heaven (must confirm with the Word of God)

Doctor

(+) Healing, gift of healing, Jesus - Great Physician

(-) Limited power, earthly solutions

(Matthew 9:12–13, Matthew 8:16–17, Mark 5:25–26, 2 Chronicles 16:12)

Father – Heavenly Father, natural father, spiritual father, generational bloodline

(Deuteronomy 32:6, Romans 8:15, Exodus 3:6)

Faceless person

(+) The Lord, angels

(-) Evil spiritual presence

(Exodus 33:20, Isaiah 6:2, Job 4:12–17)

Grandparent

(+) Spiritual inheritance / blessing, past generational issues, gift or calling to be fulfilled

(-) generational curses, undealt with generational iniquity

Husband – Jesus, the LORD, physical head (kephalē), husband in the natural / source, servant, self-sacrificial love

(Revelation 19:7, Isaiah 54:5, Ephesians 5:23-25, 28-32)

Mother – Holy Spirit, the LORD, Jesus, natural mother, spiritual mother

(Genesis 1:2, John 14:26, Isaiah 66:13, Isaiah 49:15, Matthew 23:37, John 14:26)

Past Relationships – Old issues, returning to an old way, what that person represents

Pastor

(+) Jesus Christ, shepherds in the Body, spiritual training / equipping, could represent specific ministry

(John 10:7, Jeremiah 3:15, 2 Timothy 4:2)

Police

(+) The Law, spiritual authority, angelic protection

(-) The Law, spirit of religion, false authority

(1 Peter 2:13–14, Luke 10:19, Psalm 91:11, Acts 20:28–30, Galatians 2:4, Isaiah 10:1-2)

Sibling – Fellow believer (Ephesians 4:3-6)

Brother – Jesus, brother in the natural (Hebrews 2:11, Romans 8:29)

Sister – Wisdom, the Church, sister in the natural (Proverbs 7:4, Song of Solomon 4:9-10)

Thief / Robber

(-) Enemy, false teachers, oppressive leaders

(John 10:10, 2 Peter 2:1-3, Micah 2:1-2)

Wife – Bride / Body of Christ, helper / ezer kenegdo, "a saving strength corresponding to him," wife in the natural

(Revelation 19:7, Genesis 2:18, Psalm 54:4)

PLACES

Airport

(+) Waiting on God, destiny - "destination," transition, waiting on the Holy Spirit, waiting for something to "take off"

(Isaiah 40:31, Luke 24:49, Acts 1:4-5, Psalm 105:19)

Bridge – Transition, crossing over, change of perspective, salvation

(Ephesians 2:1-5, Exodus 14:22, Acts 10:9-16)

Castle

(+) Spiritual Fortress, Name of the Lord, royalty

(-) Stronghold

(Psalm 18:2, Proverbs 18:10, Psalm 27:1, 2 Corinthians 10:3–5)

Church –Body of Christ, teaching, healing

Elevator – Rapid acceleration in spiritual growth, spirit empowered higher understanding / perspective, rapid promotion

(1 Kings 3:5–14, Isaiah 40:31, 1 Samuel 16:13, Genesis 41:14, 39-41)

Gas Station – Church/ministry for fresh infilling of the Spirit, spiritual retreat and refreshment, resting in / waiting on the Lord

(Acts 4:31, Jude 1:20, Exodus 15:27, Psalm 23: 2, Isaiah 40:31, 2 Timothy 1:6)

Gate – Spiritual authority, government, place of spiritual entrance

(Matthew 16:18, Genesis 28:17)

Grocery Store – Provision, spiritual food, variety of gifts in unity

(Philippians 4:19, 1 Corinthians 12:4–6)

Hospital – Healing / health *(note your part – patient, doctor, nurse?)*

Hotel – Temporary season

House – A person's life, legacy – Your house – current, past? *(Note which part of the house, who is there)*

Previous home – key events or issues from that time.

(Matthew 7:24–27, 1 Peter 2:5, 2 Samuel 7:16)

Attic – Generational matters

Basement – Hidden issues, spiritual foundation

Bedroom – Intimacy, rest, secret place
(Song of Solomon 1:4, Matthew 6:6)

Closet – (+) Prayer
(-) Hidden sin
(Matthew 6:6, Luke 12:3)

Dining room – Spiritual food you feed on, thanksgiving, fellowship
(1 Corinthians 10:3-4, Jeremiah 3:15, John 6:11, Acts 2:46–47, Jeremiah 3:15)

Door – (+) Jesus, opportunity, invitation, authority
(-) Missed opportunity
(1 Corinthians 16:9, Revelation 3:20, Isaiah 22:22, Matthew 25:10–12)

Garage – Where we store things - the mind, place of rest
(Romans 12:2, 1 Corinthians 2:16, Colossians 3:2)

Garden – Intimacy with God, surrender and suffering, resurrection, prosperity
(Genesis 2:8-9, Matthew 26:36, John 19:41–42, 1 Kings 4:25)

Hallway – Transition, temporary journey

Kitchen – Preparing spiritual food, teaching ministry
(Hebrews 5:12-13)

Living room – Family life, lifestyle, gathering / fellowship

Porch – Front: present to future vision, Back: vision view to the past

Windows – (+) Spiritual / prophetic vision, opportunity, letting light in, prayer (-) attack on children, thief
(Daniel 6:10, Jeremiah 9:21, Joel 2:9)

Stairs – Spiritually increasing or decreasing, heavenly activity, going up – higher level, communion, going down – decreasing, going into a time of hiddenness
(Genesis 28:12)

Yard – backyard – past; front yard - future

Restaurant

(+) Place of spiritual nourishment, church, teaching ministry *(note quality of food and cleanliness of restaurant)*

(Jeremiah 3:15, 1 Corinthians 10:3)

Roads – Life's journey, direction, ways, encounter

(+) Narrow – eternal life

(-) Broad – destruction

(Isaiah 30:2, Luke 24:13–35, Matthew 7:13–14)

School – Season of learning; elementary – foundational / elemental things, higher level – higher learning

(Hebrews 6:1-2, Luke 2:46–47, Acts 22:3)

Stadium / Arena – Large influence and reach

Theater

(+) Big picture, increased vision

(-) Hypocrite – playing a part

(Genesis 13:14-16, Matthew 15:7-9)

WEAPONS

Arrows

(+) Children, victory, person refined in hiddenness by God for powerful precise impact, prophetic words that hit the mark

(-) God's judgment on the rebellious, judgment on oppressors, attack against the upright, cruel words, lies, deception

(Psalm 127:4–5, 2 Kings 13:17, Isaiah 49:2, Deuteronomy 32:23–24, Psalm 7:12–13, Psalm 22:15, Psalm 64:3-4 & 7, Jeremiah 9:8)

Bow

(+) Supernatural strength in warfare, endurance under trials, covenant (rainbow)

(-) God's judgment for rebellion

(Psalm 18:34, Genesis 49:24, Genesis 9:13, Lamentations 2:4)

Dart

(+) Accuracy, hitting the bullseye

(-) Curse/ bitter words, attack from enemy with lasting effect, sudden destruction or consequence of sin (physical/emotional), personal attack, jealousy.

(Psalm 64:3, Ephesians 6:16, Proverbs 7:23, 1 Samuel 18:11)

Gun – Authority, powerful weapon, exerts control over others

(+) Firing at an enemy – using God-given authority

(-) Being fired at – accusation, someone using authority against you in the spiritual realm or the natural.

Knife

(+) Words, skill, discernment - cuts to the heart of a matter

(-) Gossip, slander

(Hebrews 4:12, Proverbs 12:18, Psalm 64:3)

Shield

(+) The Lord as protection, faith, protection, Word of God

(Genesis 15:1, Ephesians 6:16, Psalm 18:2, Psalm 119:114)

Spear

(+) Powerful weapon in hands of the righteous, long reaching, supernatural conquest of the powerful, redemption (in Jesus side)

(-) Threats, strong accusation, assault, jealousy

(Habakkuk 3:11, John 19:34, Psalm 57:4, 1 Samuel 18:10–11)

Sword

(+) Word of God, tongue, distinguishes soul from spirit, further reach

(-) Far reaching gossip, destructive tongue; God's judgment

(Hebrews 4:12, Psalm 57:4, Deuteronomy 32:41)

Water Gun

(+) Words empowered by the Holy Spirit, powerful influence with Spirit

(1 Corinthians 2:4-6, 1 Thessalonians 1:5)

ADDITIONAL RESOURCES

Streams Ministries – https://www.streamsministries.com

Top 20 Dreams by John Paul Jackson

The 20 Categories of Dreams based on the works of John Paul Jackson, written by Michael Wise

Dreams and Mysteries TV Series – http://dreamsandmysteries.com

God's Prophetic Symbolism in Everyday Life Visions by Adam F. Thompson and Adrian Beale

Dictionary of Biblical Imagery
Edited By: Leland Ryken, J. C. Wihoit, Tremper Longman III, By: Leland Ryken

Dream Elements: An Alternative Dream Dictionary by John E. Thomas

Unlocking Your Dreams, Autumn Mann
www.unlockingyourdreams.org
Unlocking Your Dreams PDF – https://www.unlockingyourdreams.org/wp-content/uploads/2016/04/Unlocking-Your-Dream-Student-Ma.pdf

NOTES

Chapter 1

[1]   Isaiah 61:3 For those who grieve in Zion— to bestow on them a crown of beauty instead of ashes, the oil of joy instead of mourning.

Chapter 2

[2]   2 Timothy 2:15 Be diligent to present yourself approved to God as a workman who does not need to be ashamed, accurately handling the word of truth.

[3]   Acts 17:26-27 From one man he made every nation of the human race to inhabit the entire earth, determining their set times and the fixed limits of the places where they would live, so that they would search for God and perhaps grope around for him and find him, though he is not far from each one of us.

[4]   Streams Ministries, https://streamsministries.com

[5]   Sparrow & Co., https://sparrowandco.com

Chapter 3

[6]   Ephesians 6:12 For we do not wrestle against flesh and blood, but against the rulers, against the authorities, against the cosmic powers over this present darkness, against the spiritual forces of evil in the heavenly places.

[7]   1 John 4:18 There is no fear in love, but perfect love casts out fear. For fear has to do with punishment, and whoever fears has not been perfected in love.

[8]   John 16:13 When the Spirit of truth comes, he will guide you into all the truth.

[9]   The Bema Podcast, https://www.bemadiscipleship.com

[10]   Genesis 1:5-31

[11]   Acts 2:17, 18 In the last days, God says, I will pour out my Spirit on all people Your sons and daughters will prophesy, your young men will see visions, your old men will dream dreams. Even on my servants, both men and women, I

will pour out my Spirit in those days, and they will prophesy. Exodus 33:13 If you are pleased with me, teach me your ways so I may know you and continue to find favor with you.

Chapter 4

[12] 2 Samuel 11–12

[13] Isaiah 63:5

[14] Revelation 5:10

[15] 2 Corinthians 5:18, 19

[16] Matthew 4:4

[17] John 10:10 The thief comes only to steal and kill and destroy; I came so that they would have life and have *it* abundantly.

[18] "Man and His Symbols," by Carl Jung, published in 1968 by Dell Publishing. "I have made it a rule to remind myself that I can never understand somebody else's dream well enough to interpret it correctly."

[19] Genesis 40:8; Daniel 2:28

[20] A continuationist is a Christian who believes that the Holy Spirit's gifts, or spiritual gifts, are still in use today. These gifts include healings, tongues, miracles, prophecy, and interpretation of tongues. Continuationists believe that these gifts have been in operation since the Day of Pentecost and are still needed to strengthen and build up the church.

[21] Genesis 40:8 And they said to him, We each have had a dream, and *there is* no interpreter of it. So Joseph said to them, Do not interpretations belong to God? Tell *them* to me, please.

[22] Daniel 2:17-19

Chapter 5

[23] Hebrews 13:8 Jesus Christ is the same yesterday and today and forever.

[24] James 1:17 Every good thing given and every perfect gift is from above, coming down from the Father of lights, with whom there is no variation or shifting shadow.

[25] Job 33:15-18 In a dream, in a vision of the night, when deep sleep falls on people as they slumber in their beds, he may speak in their ears and terrify them with warnings, to turn them from wrongdoing and keep them from pride, to preserve them from the pit, their lives from perishing by the sword.

[26] Matthew 2:12 And having been warned in a dream not to go back to Herod, they returned to their country by another route.

27   Daniel 4:17 Renounce your sins by doing what is right, and your wickedness by being kind to the oppressed. It may be that then your prosperity will continue.

28   James 1:17 Every good thing given and every perfect gift is from above, coming down from the Father of lights, with whom there is no variation or shifting shadow.

29   John 10:10 The thief comes only to steal and kill and destroy; I came so that they would have life and have it abundantly.

30   Zechariah 10:2

31   2 Timothy 1:7

32   James 4:6 God opposes the proud but gives grace to the humble. 1 Peter 5:5 Clothe yourselves, all of you, with humility toward one another, for "God opposes the proud but gives grace to the humble."

33   Philippians 4:6,7 Be anxious for nothing, but in everything by prayer and supplication with thanksgiving let your requests be made know to God. and the peace of God which surpasses all comprehension, will guard your hearts and your minds in Christ Jesus.

34   James 4:7 So be subject to God. Resist the devil [stand firm against him], and he will flee from you. AMP

35   Proverbs 18:10 The name of the Lord is a strong tower; the righteous run to it and are safe.

Chapter 6

36   Lisa Kratz Thomas and Kathy Gray, "Light in our Darkness: Deception, Murder and Unexpected Grace," Cappella Books, 2016

37   Wise, Michael, "The 20 Categories of Dreams, Understanding the Various Ways God Speaks through Dreams, Based on the works of John Paul Jackson" Streams Ministries International, 2021

38   Ecclesiastes 5:3 For a dream comes with much business and painful effort, and a fool's voice with many words.

39   Ecclesiastes 5:12 The sleep of a laboring man is sweet, whether he eats little or much, but the fullness of the rich will not let him sleep.

Chapter 7

40   Matthew 7:17 Ask and it will be given to you; seek and you will find; knock and the door will be opened to you.

Chapter 8

[41] 1 John 1:0 If we confess our sins, he is faithful to forgive us our sins and cleanse us from all unrighteousness. James 4:16 ...confess your sins to one another, and pray for one another, so that you may be healed. The effective prayer of a righteous man can accomplish much.

[42] Matthew 18:3-4 And He called a child to Himself and set him among them, and said, "Truly I say to you, unless you change and become like children, you will not enter the kingdom of heaven."

Chapter 10

[43] During normal waking life.

[44] Hebrews 11:22 By faith Joseph, when he was dying, made mention of the departure of the children of Israel, and gave instructions concerning his bones.

[45] Genesis 50:24, 25 Then Joseph said to his brothers, 'I am about to die. But God will surely come to your aid and take you up out of this land to the land he promised on oath to Abraham, Isaac and Jacob.' And Joseph made the Israelites swear an oath and said, 'God will surely come to your aid, and then you must carry my bones up from this place.'

[46] Genesis 41:32 The dream was repeated to Pharaoh twice because the thing is established by God, and God will shortly bring it to pass.

Chapter 11

[47] Isaiah 61:1-4

[48] Romans 8:1 Therefore, there is now no condemnation for those who are in Christ Jesus.

[49] Psalm 139:16 All the days ordained for me were written in your book before one of them came to be.139:16

[50] Ephesians 6:18 Praying at all times in the Spirit, with all prayer and supplication. To that end, keep alert with all perseverance, making supplication for all the saints. ESV

[51] John 10:10 The thief comes only to steal and kill and destroy; I have come that they may have life and have it to the full.

[52] Hebrews 1:14 Are not all angels ministering spirits sent to serve those who will inherit salvation?

[53] 2 Peter 1:3-4 His divine power has given us everything we need for life and godliness, through the knowledge of Him who called us by His own glory and virtue. NLT

[54]   1 Corinthians 16:14

Chapter 12

[55]   Psalm 3:3 But You, LORD, are a shield around me, My glory, and the One who lifts my head. NASB; Romans 8:31 What then shall we say to these things? If God is for us, who can be against us? ESV; Isaiah 26:3 You will keep in perfect peace all who trust in you, all whose thoughts are fixed on you. NLT

[56]   James 5:16 ...confess your sins to each other and pray for each other so that you may be healed.

[57]   Matthew 5:23–24 Therefore, if you are offering your gift at the altar and there remember that your brother or sister has something against you, leave your gift there in front of the altar. First go and be reconciled to them; then come and offer your gift.

Chapter 13

[58]   Ephesians 6:12

[59]   Ephesians 4:15, 16 Instead, speaking the truth in love, we will grow to become in every respect the mature body of him who is the head, that is, Christ, from him the whole body, joined and held together by every supporting ligament, grows and builds itself up in love, as each part does its work. NIV

[60]   1 Samuel 3:3-18

[61]   Deuteronomy 7:5, 6a You shall tear down their altars, smash their memorial stones, cut their Asherim to pieces, and burn their carved images in the fire. For you are a holy people to the Lord your God.

[62]   James 1:5 If anyone lacks wisdom, let him ask God and he will be given it.

[63]   Ephesians 6:12 For we do not wrestle against flesh and blood, but against the rulers, against the authorities, against the cosmic powers over this present darkness, against the spiritual forces of evil in the heavenly places.

[64]   Ephesians 6:18 Praying at all times in the Spirit, with all prayer and supplication. To that end, keep alert with all perseverance, making supplication for all the saints.

[65]   2 Samuel 3:39b The LORD shall repay the evildoer according to his wickedness.

Chapter 14

[66] 1 John 3:15 Anyone who hates a brother or sister is a murderer.

[67] The Remnant Radio, https://www.theremnantradio.com

Chapter 15

[68] J. G. Thompson, The New Bible Dictionary, (Grand Rapids: Eerdmans Pub. Co., 1978), pp. 1312-1313

[69] Strong's Exhaustive Concordance of the Bible, James Strong, 1890, Cincinnati: Jennings & Graham.

[70] Exodus 3:1-10, Genesis 12:1-3, 1 Kings 19:11-13, 1 Samuel 3:1-10, Isaiah 6:1-8

[71] Acts 12:13-15

Chapter 16

[72] John 10:10 The enemy comes only to steal, kill and destroy; But I have come that you may have life, and have it abundantly.

[73] Ezekiel 8:3, Ezekiel 37:1, John 6:21, Acts 8:38-40, 2 Corinthians 12:2-4

[74] Genesis 3:5 For God knows that when you eat from it your eyes will be opened, and you will be like God, knowing good and evil.

[75] John 10:1, 10 Truly, truly, I say to you, he who does not enter the sheepfold by the door but climbs in by another way, that man is a thief and a robber. The thief comes only to steal and kill and destroy. I came that they may have life and have it abundantly.

[76] Revelation 12:11 And they overcame him by the blood of the Lamb and by the word of their testimony.

[77] John 14:16-17 He shall give you another Comforter, that he may abide with you forever; even the Spirit of truth.

[78] Luke 10:19 Behold, I have given you authority to tread on serpents and scorpions, and over all the power of the enemy, and nothing shall hurt you.

[79] Galatians 5:16-24

[80] Ephesians 2:10

[81] Deuteronomy 31:6 "Be strong and courageous. Do not be afraid or terrified because of them, for the Lord your God goes with you; he will never leave you nor forsake you."

Chapter 17

[82] Colossians 2:8 See to it that no one takes you captive through hollow and deceptive philosophy, which depends on human tradition and the elemental

spiritual forces of this world rather than on Christ.; 1 Corinthians 15:33 Do not be misled: 'Bad company corrupts good character.'. Galatians 1:6-7 I am astonished that you are so quickly deserting the one who called you… and are turning to a different gospel… Evidently some people are throwing you into confusion and are trying to pervert the gospel of Christ.; 2 Timothy 3:13 Evil people and impostors will go from bad to worse, deceiving and being deceived.

83 John 16:3 But when He, the Spirit of truth comes, He will guide you into all truth. NASB

84 "Navigating Insights: The Wit & Wisdom of Skip Gray," by Skip and Buzzie Gray, p. 73, Skipper Publishing, copyright 2015

Chapter 18

85 John Paul Jackson, Fireside Chat Episode 21, 2004

86 Streams Ministries offers many resources from quick reference cards to books on common dreams and categories, to entire courses on dream interpretation. Other resources that we have found trustworthy are listed in the appendix.

87 James 3:7,8 For every kind of beast and bird, of reptile and sea creature, can be tamed and has been tamed by mankind, but no human being can tame the tongue.

Chapter 20

88 Psalm 4:8 In peace I will both lie down and sleep, for You alone, O Lord, make me to dwell in safety; Psalm 127:1,2 Unless the Lord builds the house, they labor in vain who build it; Unless the Lord guards the city, the watchman keeps awake in vain. It is vain for you to rise up early to retire late, to eat the bread of painful labors; for He gives to His beloved even in his sleep.

89 Psalm 91

90 Ephesians 1:17-19 I keep asking that the God of our Lord Jesus Christ, the glorious Father, may give you the Spirit of wisdom and revelation, so that you may know him better. I pray that the eyes of your heart may be enlightened in order that you may know the hope to which he has called you, the riches of his glorious inheritance in his holy people, and his incomparably great power for us who believe.

ABOUT THE AUTHOR

Kathy Gray is the author of *Light In Our Darkness*, a speaker, mentor, and former radio talk show host whose life is marked by a deep commitment to helping others hear the voice of God—especially through dreams and visions. Raised in a Biblically grounded, academically rich ministry home, she has spent more than two decades studying biblical dream interpretation. For the past eight years, she has developed and taught dream interpretation seminars— primarily within evangelical circles— equipping men and women to discern God's voice with greater clarity, humility, and confidence.

Outside of writing and teaching, Kathy spends her days enjoying her family, investing in and receiving from the spiritual community God has placed around her, mentoring others, and playing and teaching piano. She is devoted to discovering and living out every way God reveals Himself through His Word.

Originally from Colorado, Kathy and her husband, Dave, have called Highland Village, Texas, home for the past 28 years. Their four grown sons also live and work in the Dallas area. The men in her family are avid golfers and hit the links together as often as they can. Kathy loves to escape to the Rocky Mountains relishing time outside in their beauty and crisp, thin air—preferably with Dave—along with a stash of dark chocolate in hand.

To schedule Kathy for speaking engagements, email Kathy@ KathyGrayMinistries.org

Kathy Gray Ministries Website:
Kathygrayministries.org

QR code

https://kathygrayministries.org